Architectural Supermodels
physical design simulation

Tom Porter & John Neale

Architectural Press

OXFORD   **AUCKLAND**   **BOSTON**   **JOHANNESBURG**   **MELBOURNE**   **NEW DELHI**

Architectural Press
An imprint of Butterworth-Heinemann
Linacre House, Jordan Hill, Oxford OX2 8DP
225 Wildwood Avenue, Woburn, MA 01801-2041
A division of Reed Educational and Professional Publishing Ltd

ℛ A member of the Reed Elsevier plc group

First published 2000

British Library Cataloguing in Publication Data
Porter, Tom
  Architectural supermodels: physical design simulation
   1. Architectural models 2. Architectural models - computer
   aided design 3. Architectural - Data processing
   I. Title II. Neale, John

   ISBN 0 7506 4928 3

Library of Congress Cataloguing in Publication Data
A catalogue record for this book is available from the Library of Congress

Layout design: John Neale

 For Holly, Siena and Gianluca

Printed and bound in Great Britain

Contents

ACKNOWLEDGEMENTS

The authors also would like to thank the following for the generous help and encouragement by supplying text and material:

Richard Armiger, Chris Barber, Alan Brookes, Donnathea Campbell, Mike Cash, Michael Cook, Jon Courtney-Thompson, Roderick Coyne, Siân Cryer, Alan Davidson, Andrea Day, George Dombek, Terry Farrell, Jack Forman, Debbie Gibbs, David Gomm, Romaine Govett, Katy Harris, Ron Hess, Andrew Ingham, Basil Kalaitzis, Ian Latham, Conway Lloyd-Morgan, Katherine MacInnes, Ian Maddocks, Martin Markcrow, Keith Mendenhall, Henk Mihl, Byron Mikellides, Keith H. Palmer, Michael Pawlyn, Paolo Pellandini, Stephen Pimbley, Andrew Putler, Paul Proundman, Adrian Robinson, Richard Rose-Casemore, Toby Shew, Don Shuttleworth, Pauline Sones, Holly Spiegel, Hannah Stone, Keith Styles, Robert Tavernor, Catherine Tranmer, Bernard Tschumi, Matthew Wells, Tina Wilson, Nicole Woodman, Vlassis Vellios and Ademir Volic.

The authors would also like to pay special thanks to Edward Woodman.

BIBLIOGRAPHY

Botta, M,   *Mario Botta: Public Buildings,* Skira Editore, Milan,1998

Busch, A,   *The Art of the Architectural Model,* Design Press, New York, 1990

Davidson, A,   'My Computers', *Architects' Journal*, Oct.,1994

Glancey, J,   'You Are About to Enter a New Dimension: a Journey Through the Frontiers of Gallery Design', *The Guardian,* 8 March, 1999

Fisher, T,   *Communicating Ideas Artfully*, Steelcase Design Partnership, New York, 1990

Janke, R,   *Architectural Models*, Academy Editions, London,1978

Jones, A M,   *Technoart,* Chromopark issue, Localiser 11,Gestalten-Verl., Berlin,1996

Lloyd Morgan, C,
& Zampi, Z,   *Virtual Architecture*, Batsford, London, 1995

LeCuyer, A,   'Designs of the Computer', *The Architectural Review*, London, 1995

Linton, H,   *Colour Model Environments*, Van Nostrand Reinhold, New York, 1985

Massie, W E,   'The Implications of Corporal Occupation of a Virtual Construct', *Architecture*, April, 1998

Neale, J W,   *Supermodels*, Diploma disseration, School of Architecture, Oxford Brookes University, 1998

Mosser, M,   'Models of French Architecture in the Age of Enlightenment', *Daidalos,* Berlin, December, 1981

Parkyn, P,   'A Model Briefing Package', *Architects' Journal*, pp. 24-26, 1992

Porter, T,   *How Architects Visualise*, Studio Vista, London, 1979

Porter, T,   *The Architect's Eye,* Chapman & Hall, London, 1997

Tavernor, R,   'Architects' and Historians' Models', *Society of Architectural Historians of Great Britain*, No. 53, London, 1998

Tavernor, R,   *On Alberti and the Art of Building*, Yale University Press, New Haven, 1998

Trudeau, N,   *Professional Modelmaking*, Whitney Library of Design, New York, 1995

INTRODUCTION

In the face of the digital revolution and despite its hitherto rather humdrum image, modelmaking has made a recent and massive comeback in the world of environmental design. Indeed, according to the results of two recent surveys that canvassed the top ten requirements of architectural and interior design employers, the ability to visualise directly in three dimensions and to construct models, together with abilities in freehand and technical drawing and literacy in computer graphics, remain among the top five skills required by the modern architectural practice from their prospective employees.

Furthermore, during the last few years the activity of modelmaking has moved away from the ubiquitous all-white model and the highly-detailed presentation model. Also, influential architects, such as Frank Gehry, Nigel Coates and Will Alsop employ models that now express an immediacy and a much more profound and exciting design dimension, i.e., an architectural language that cannot be readily experienced via drawings alone. Moreover, despite their reputation for dynamic drawings and renderings, the studios of Zaha Hadid, Daniel Libeskind and Steven Holl use the model as a conduit for exploring embryonic ideas. Models exist at the heart of their design thinking, a single project sometimes being subjected to literally scores of sequentially built exploratory maquettes, each made in order to refine and resolve function and form and, of course, to increase the buildability of their concepts.

Architectural Supermodels traces the life and roles of the physical model from design process maquettes to their transformation and proliferation in the two-dimensional 'reality' of a photograph and, again, their metamorphosis in cyberspace as a digital model. This newly developed relationship between the physical model and the computer is of great interest. The fact that a three-dimensional model can now be electronically modified, refined, and digitally transformed back into a new physical existence brings a new and exciting dimension to the design previewing skill of the architect. Also of interest are advances in computer technology that now hold the potential for allowing the designer to move directly from concept to full-scale construction

Developed from the theme of a dissertation by John Neale while a Diploma student under the supervision of Dr Murray Fraser at the School of Architecture, Oxford Brookes University, *Architectural Supermodels* is written in the spirit of this mood change and in the notion of exploring more exciting ways of expressing design concepts. It also celebrates the work and contribution of many of the unsung originators of physical models whose input and identities often remain hidden behind the reputation of the architectural practices that commission them. Furthermore, *Architectural Supermodels* argues not for those immaculately crafted, prohibitively expensive and professionally built miniaturisations that appear simply to impress the client or the public but for those built unashamedly as tools for engaging disputed aspects of design. Indeed, supermodels are those that directly address those factors that have impact on the outcome of our future environment.

1

A Short History

'From the beginning, the dual function of the model emerges. On the one hand it serves the creative process and on the other hand it is supposed to be an immediate comprehensible means of communication with non- specialists.' **Monique Mosser**

There has always been a fascination with the idea of physically miniaturising both fictitious and planned architectural projects as a means of previewing their impact at full-scale. While the decoding of architectural drawing, especially orthographic drawings, requires a certain amount of knowledge and experience, the physical scale model is a tool that, albeit diminuative, can instantly convey the form and the 'feel' of a building. Therefore, scaled down representations of objects and buildings have, in one form or another, and to serve different purposes, been in existence since the dawn of antiquity (fig. 1.1). Originally used as offerings placed in tombs, the ancient gods were once their only recipients and sole observers. But, as history unfolds, the gods came to be be superseded by the designer, the client and the architectural tutor.

fig. 1.1 Chinese pottery tomb offering (1st - 2nd century BC).

The architectural models of Greek and Roman antiquity, if they existed at all, are known only from literature. The oldest acknowledged architectural model is mentioned in Herodotus, who describes a model of the Delphi Temple in his writing (Herodotus V, 62). However, the notion that the early builders worked directly from maquettes is deemed unlikely by the majority of modern archaeologists and historians. This is because the ancient Greeks, and the Egyptians before them, primarily built their temples and mausoleums in relation to their sacred canons before any thought of pleasing their own aesthetic sensibilities. Indeed, if only half of modern theorists are correct, the Great Pyramid, Stonehenge, the Parthenon and other ancient monuments were designed and constructed exclusively according to scientific needs; their location, setting, size and geometry being determined by the need to embody cosmic measures and ratios. For instance, it is unlikely that the ancient Greek designers worked from scaled models because, within a technology lacking fine measurement, models for such massive structures would have led to inaccuracies in their construction.

A striving for precision in the widespread repetition of architectural components appears to have been more central to their visualisation of space. If it is accepted that the Greek architect designed against proven proportional systems (for these existed long before their philosophical theories had been elaborated by the Pythagoreans), it is likely that rules were formulated in such a way that they were 'portable', i.e., being applied as the building went up, with little detailed design beforehand. Furthermore, the archaeologist J.J. Coulton suggests that there is considerable evidence of 'paradeigmata', full-scale specimens of the more detailed building components, such as capitals. From these mock-ups builders could extract detailed dimensions with callipers, thereby achieving repetition from replicas without any need for scaling up or conversions.

Until well into the Middle Ages, architectural space was developed in this way. For instance, according to Christopher Alexander the medieval architect would take long journeys - even travelling abroad - in order to study and measure the essential proportions of 'full-sized specimens,' buildings which had been admired and selected by his or her patron for adaptation. The later introduction of a wooden scale model served only to communicate his intentions to the client and also extract a detailed estimate of cost. By the end of the Gothic period models of parts of buildings were being made, possibly for testing purposes. One form of model-making used as a design tool was the paper cut-out, which could demonstrate patterns of vaulting ribs and be bent by the medieval designer in order to simulate the intended structure of a space.

By contrast, his Renaissance counterpart had no such sure frame of reference as he was bent on an architecture inspired by a rubble of Graeco-Roman components, the apparent success of which was to provide a design-kit *par excellence* for the next five centuries. The only way he or she could test the feasibility of these more dynamic visions was to build exploratory working models, sometimes in the actual building materials intended for use. Therefore, the earliest known architectural models originated in the mid-fourteenth century in the context of new architectural concepts based upon a comprehensive planning process. It was, therefore, common practice to develop architectural concepts in the round by constructing large prefabrications in wood, plaster and clay. These were not used purely for structural experiment as in the Middle Ages but, often utilising ingenious pull-away sections and detachable roofs and floors for internal viewing, functioned as design aids in the simulated penetration of light and the visual orchestration of mass and space.

If, indeed, the scale model functioned as a design overture before the Italian Renaissance, then it was to achieve a new status during the Quattrocento when the concept of the architect as sole creator and controller of building design was developed. A wide range of specialised models were used in the creation of major undertakings, such as Filippo Brunelleschi's and Michelangelo's respective scaled prefabrications for the dome of Florence Cathedral and St Peter's, Rome (fig. 1.2). In *Vita di Brunelleschi, c.* 1482-9, Antonio di Tuccio Manetti touches on his use of models. Manetti also describes how Brunelleschi, during the building of the dome, communicated complex structural configurations to his puzzled stonemasons. To do so, he made expanatory models for them ' . . . in soft clay and then in wax and wood. Actually those large turnips, called goblets, which come on the market in winter were useful for making the small models and for explaining things to them'. Brunelleschi primarily invented in three dimensions and sometimes built his preparatory constructions to 1/12th of their proposed scale. His wooden design model of the dome and apse section survives still, as does possibly the largest and most spectacular Renaissance model ever made: Antonio da Sangallo's aborted design for St. Peter's in Rome. Commissioned in 1539 and made to the scale of 1/24th of the full size, it took several years to make and is still to be seen in the Vatican Museum. Leon Battista Alberti called for the 'use of scale models to examine every part of a proposal'; his *Ten Books on Architecture* contain a description of the type of model he found useful in his design process. He writes: 'I would not have the model too exactly finished, not too delicate and neat, but plain and simple - more to be admired for the contrivance of the inventor than the hand of the workman.' It is known that the great Renaissance architects have more than once had models made of the same size as the building, or at least especially important parts, particularly those that would repeat themselves within the building. Bernini used this technique for the colonnades of St. Peter's Square and Michelangelo temporarily mounted a false crown on the Palazzo Farnese. These occasional full-size prefabrications were enlisted as a visual check and, in conjunction with scale models and drawings, came to provide the ultimate vehicle on which final design decisions were made. In a letter to Vasari complaining of a structural collapse which had occurred during construction of one his projects, Michelangelo explained that it had arisen, ' . . . even though I had made an exact model, as I always do.' Vasari also documented Michelangelo's design sequence for the cupola of St. Peter's in Rome which began with a clay model along with plan and section sketches; this initial phase led to the construction of a large wooden model, which took two years to complete, through which its final form was achieved.

fig. 1.2 Michelangelo's model of the cupola for St. Peter's, Rome.

The significance of the model in this period can be seen in this painting by Domenico Cresti (also known as Passignano) painted in 1620 and entitled 'Michelangelo Shows Pope Paul IV the Model of the Dome of St. Peter's'. Here we see the architect marketing the design of the basilica of St. Peter's using the physical power and seductive presence of his large wooden model (fig. 1.3). We also see the supermodel in action for the first time; the apparent high quality of its workmanship clearly intended to indicate through its detail, structure and form how the building could, in reality, exist. Furthermore, the model provides the focal point of a discussion involving a committee of powerful clients, who will judge the merits of the design against, albeit reduced in scale, clear evidence of its physical existence. Henceforth, the physical model was to provide a powerful means of communicating and promoting the form of an architectural proposition; as well, of course, as functioning as an exploratory design tool.

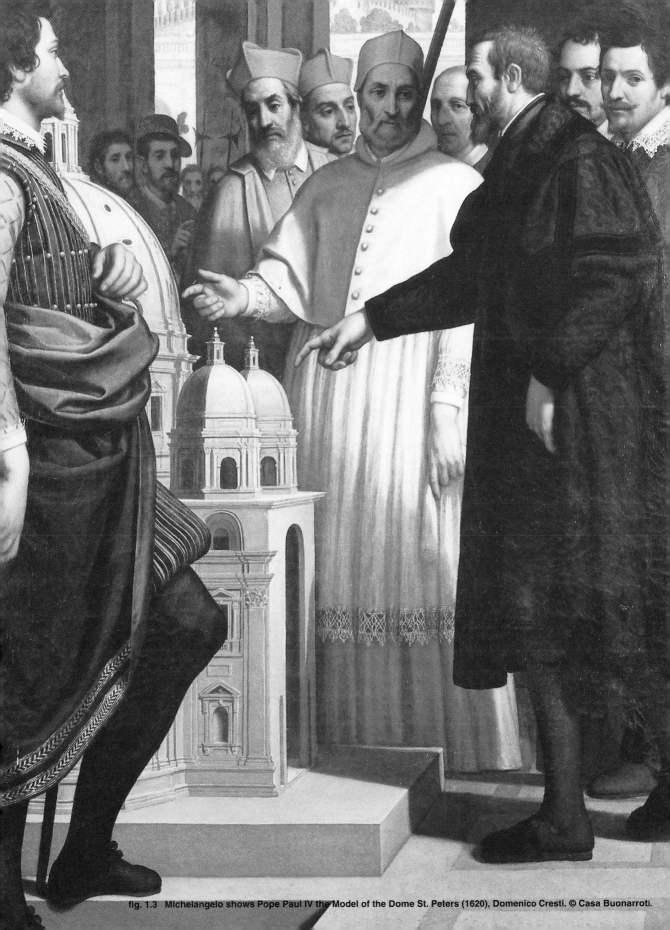

fig. 1.3 Michelangelo shows Pope Paul IV the Model of the Dome St. Peters (1620), Domenico Cresti. © Casa Buonarroti.

By the sixteenth century, while the architect began to shed his creative dialogue with three dimensions and work almost entirely with graphic means, the model began to assume a different role. It had become an explanatory device rather than an exploratory tool. Undoubtedly, it was Sangallo's giant wooden model which, in the seventeenth century, was to inspire Sir Christopher Wren to render his ideal design for the new St. Paul's in this way. Between 1673 and 1674 a team of craftsmen under the supervision of William and Richard Cleer constructed the Great Model for Wren at a cost of £600. It was executed with the greatest accuracy to the scale of 1 inch to 1'- 6" and it is possible to walk inside this 18 foot high object, which is still in the possession of the Cathedral (figs. 1.4a & 1.4b). However, Wren considered the model to be less for his own benefit than for that of builders or client. He wrote that 'a good and careful large model' should be constructed for 'the encouragement and satisfaction of the benefactors who comprehend not designs and drafts on paper.' As an adjunct to a visualisation process in which drawing had become a language of the initiated, the new role of model-making represented a step away from any holistic conceptualisation of form and space. This shift in emphasis was reflected in the high degree of finish of models and was contemporaneous with a movement towards the communication of external appearance for its own sake. For instance, during construction of St. Paul's Wren had plaster full-size copies of pieces of sculpture intended for its facade positioned on the unfinished edifice in order to examine its visual effect and as a check on its scale prior to their ultimate realisation in stone.

fig. 1.4a

fig. 1.4b

Interior views of the Great Model for St. Paul's Cathedral. By permission of the Dean and Chapter of St. Paul's Cathedral.

Wren's use of full-scale prefabrications for previewing architectural components *in situ* is a technique that simply replicates one already well-rehearsed in the design processes of Michelanglo and Bernini. It was well-established in the Age of Enlightenment especially in France where 'maquette-makers' still clung on to some superiority over 'perspective drawers'. Evidence of this is found in the section on 'usefulness of various models of significant buildings' in Blondel's *Cours de'architecture,* 1774. Under the classical axiom 'one can be a good draftsman and still understand nothing about the art of building', Blondel describes three types of model. First, there is the scaled model of the complete building design, its function being to communicate with the client. However, its scale limitation as a design aid should be augmented by two further types: one is the full-size prototype of architectural elements - built to ensure perfection in the preview of important and repetitive parts of the building; another is intended for use during actual construction. The latter functions as a full-size mock-up of decorative detail such as capitals, entablature and sculpture, etc., 'which must be placed on the right spot of the building in order to judge the effect'. This circumvented the inherent perceptual problem associated with reduced models in which ' . . . the eye perceives with ease what it incompletely sees when the building is finished'.

Examples of a more illusionistic version of the full-size model is found in the work of architect Soufflot in France during the same period. There is evidence that when designing a house for a private client, he 'had the draft of the facade drawn to full size in front of the old buildings on a plaster rough-cast that he had ordered for the purpose'. It is also known that in 1767 he made a same-size stucco model of one half of the facade protrusion of the Hôtel des Monnaies. Installed on its intended site for public and client approval on the Left Bank of the Seine, the object measured 15 metres high and 13 metres wide. But perhaps the most daring project of all was his creation in 1764 of a virtual replica of an as yet unbuilt architecture. This used painted picture screens stretched over a three-dimensional timber framework to simulate the appearance of St. Geneviève church in Paris. This theatrical use of part model, part image - with its *trompe l'oeil* portal painted by the artist, Pierre-Antoine De Machy - was created so that the attendant throng and Louis XV, while laying its foundation stone, could appreciate, albeit as an optical illusion, the full spatial and polychromatic effect of the interior and facades of the future church. This illusionistic event, possibly the first of its kind to give a full-scale visibility to non-existence, was also recorded two-dimensionally in an oil painting by De Machy (fig. 1.5).

fig.1.5   Painted canvas replica of St. Geneviève Church, Paris recorded in 1764 in an oil painting by Pierre-Antoine De Machy. © Marie de Paris.

During the mid-eighteenth century and coincident with the newly founded technical colleges, the teaching model flourished. These simulated more complex structural and constructional situations and were used in the instruction of technical students, building trade journeymen and also in the education of officers serving in the engineer corps. Meanwhile, architectural models of the period were made of timber, plaster, cardboard or talc; the latter produced from gypsum and not to be confused with normal plaster of Paris. Talc was preferred for its aesthetic qualities, i.e., because it presented a finish that better simulated stone. In the early nineteenth century these were joined by paste-board and cork when, apart from the fashion for modelling buildings of antiquity, models continued to be used for any major undertaking. But, with the growth of the print medium and the introduction of specialised architectural drawings, virtuoso draftsmanship and especially coloured artist's impressions with emotive lighting and tricks of scale, the central role of models began to decline. For any major public building, however, such as those for the Houses of Parliament and the Law Courts, competition required

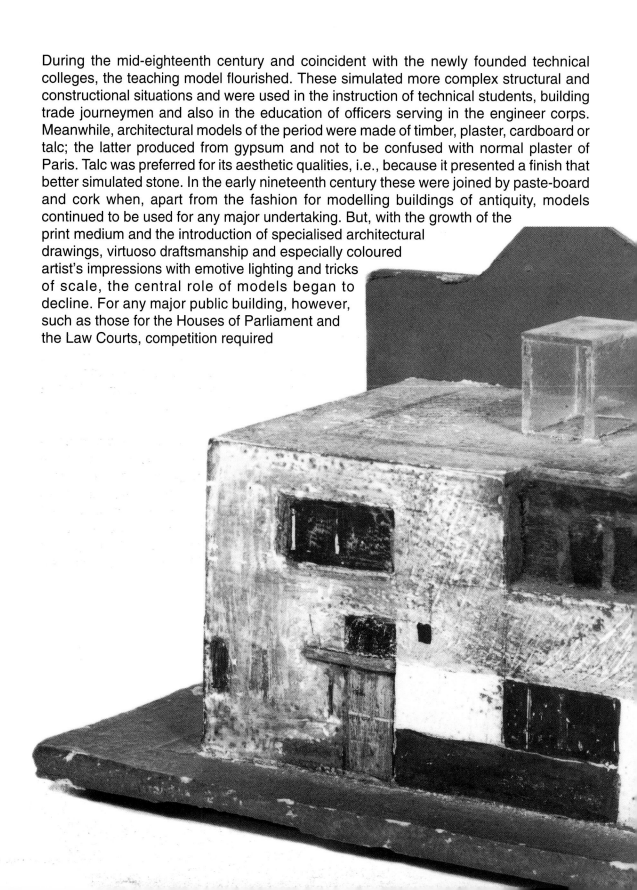

models to be exhibited for public debate as well as informed comment. The architect's use for these models properly comes to an end with the completion of the building. Although many of these display models were recorded in photographs, they proved extremely vulnerable, and many have perished. Indeed, like the end-of-term ceremonial destruction of models by architectural students, Brunelleschi, in a reported fit of frustration, is supposed to have smashed the elaborate model he prepared for the Palazzo Medici. Consequently, when they do survive they provide a retrospective insight of architects' spatial anticipations and, in themselves, can become celebrated as treasured relics.

However, in rebelling against the remoteness of paper designs from the real world of work, Walter Gropius founded the Bauhaus in 1919 and devised its revolutionary curriculum in the hope of resurrecting the medieval 'lost chord' between designer and craftsman. Although its programme included the study of plane geometry and drafting techniques one tutor, Laszlo Moholy-Nagy - a Constructivist with a predilection for the dynamics of light - encouraged his students to employ as a design tool a simple, partly transparent model which he called a 'space modulator'. He explained that this was intended to provide them with an opportunity of relating concepts to materials 'as against previous architectural methods in which structural interventions were hampered by the short-comings of visualisation on paper alone'.

Consequently, the supermodel seems to have re-established itself as a vital design tool at the beginning of the twentieth century. Indeed, it was to play a significant role in witnessing the birth pangs of countless built and unbuilt Modernist icons. For instance, there was Gerrit Reitveld's search for a new, polychromatic and pure plastic order in his sequence of Schröder House models (fig.1.6) . . .

fig. 1.6   Gerrit Reitveld's first model of the Schröder House. Collection: Centraal Museum, Utrecht.

fig. 1.7 Vladimir Tatlin's model for his Monument to the Third International.
Courtesy: British Architectural Library, RIBA, London.

. . . and Vladimir Tatlin's quest for a monumental metaphor for the harmony of a new social order expressed in the huge Monument to the Third International model of his leaning, twin helicoidal tower (fig. 1.7). There was also Adolf Loos' models that grappled with his critical and lyrical attempt to combine Platonic mass with irregular volume.

Largely responsible for English classical revivalism, Sir Edwin Lutyens' design for Liverpool's Roman Catholic Cathedral of 1929-1944 represented the culmination of a distinguished architectural career. Although only the crypt was built, Lutyens' model of his design is one of the most important surviving supermodels in Britain after the one for Wren's St. Paul's (fig.1.8). Built by J.P. Thorp model-makers and taking twelve craftsmen two years to make, the 17 foot long and over 11 foot high wooden model was the sensation of the 1934 Royal Academy Summer Exhibition. Indeed, more recently Sir John Summerson has written: 'The question whether a building can assume a place of authority in the world of architecture without actually being built is a curious one; but the answer is not in doubt. Bramante's design for St. Peter's dome and Wren's great model for St. Paul's still pull their weight in the history books and a whole treatise could be written on the influence of Bernini's rejected design for the Louvre. Lutyens' cathedral, no less than these, is a landmark in the architectural history of its time.' If built, Lutyens' Cathedral would have been much larger than St. Paul's and only slightly smaller than St. Peter's, but its greatness lay less in its size than its grandeur of purpose and conception.

In this context it is worth mentioning the design approach of Anton Gaudi, a designer of unquestionable genius whose visualisation methods were as unconventional as his architectural forms. His designs for the Church at Santa Coloma and the Sagrada Familia in Barcelona did not include graphic techniques but were evolved through a series of inverted wire and canvas models, worked out with the engineer Eduardo Goetz, and the sculptor Bertran. He rarely drew plans and relied almost exclusively upon three-dimensional forms of visualisation - a method which, rather than inhibiting creativity, increased his capacity for articulating highly complex space. Gaudi's grasp of space was reinforced by workshop experience and a feel for materials which echoed that of the medieval architects.

It is this essential grasp of materials and space that marks off the important early twentieth-century architects as creative designers who visualise and articulate their concepts in an imaginative and unconventional manner. A random study of their formative experience and design methods discloses a conceptual process which, being founded upon an understanding of the potential of space in all its manifestations, transcends a singular reliance upon drawing. For example, in the book *Eero Saarinen on His Own Work*, he describes his own visualisation process which replicates that of Michelangelo by first modelling space in clay before any graphic interpretation. Saarinen explains that the plasticity of the form of his TWA Terminal in New York's JFK Airport could not have been achieved on paper alone. A break with the rigidity of graphics we associate with traditional drafting is embodied in the highly expressive drawings of Louis Kahn. Although himself a master draftsman. he discovered that, when faced with complex forms, a graphic visualisation can reach a redundancy point. For example, Kahn encountered the futility of perspective views when in association with Ann Tyng and whilst attempting to draw the complicated structure of tetrahedrons of their project for the Philadelphia City Hall, he turned instead to the modelmaking medium.

fig. 1.8 Sir Edwin Lutyens' model of his proposed design for Liverpool Metropolitan Cathedral. Courtesy: Board of Trustees of the National Museums and Galleries on Merseyside(Walker Art Gallery, Liverpool).

However, those models that survive the ravages of time, rejection and inadequate storage represent a rich archive that catalogues all those unbuilt, drastically modified or demolished structures from the past and near past. Indeed, until recently we could see a reconstruction of Tatlin's Monument to the Third International in London, and Mies's Mile High skyscraper in New York's Museum of Modern Art, etc. There are also those controversial competition winners (and, indeed, celebrated losers) whose unrealised architecture - often due to committee shortsightedness - remain trapped forever in their diminuitive existence. If not themselves destroyed, many important models have disappeared into private hands as objects of decoration. For instance, lamenting the loss of some design models for the 1951 Festival of Britain complex, Richard Armiger of The Network modelmakers - tasked with restoring those that had survived - suggested that the missing Skylon model could be out there somewhere sitting on someone's mantelpiece. However, one Festival of Britain model that survives is the late Sir Basil Spence's maquette of The Museum of the Ship (fig. 1.9).

As we shall see, however, apart from those created for the client and public consumption, physical models are created at different scales and in different degrees of finish within the design process to fulfil a variety of functions.

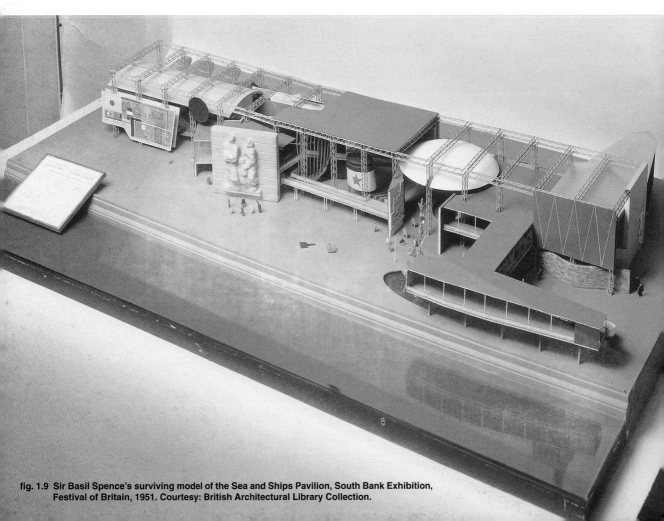

fig. 1.9 Sir Basil Spence's surviving model of the Sea and Ships Pavilion, South Bank Exhibition, Festival of Britain, 1951. Courtesy: British Architectural Library Collection.

2

Role Models

'Models can appear in different roles along the process of creating architecture. As designs unfold, models tend to progressively increase in scale and detail, each successive model taking us ever closer to the design resolution.' David Gomm, Kandor Modelmakers Ltd

Within the process of architectural design, the model can represent an essential tool in the realisation of habitable built form. Making a model is about as close as one can get to the actual construction of a design idea, and can be used for a variety of different functions. For example, in the investigation of interior and exterior form, structure, colour, surface and lighting, etc. Above all, however, models can help with the creative process of visualising three-dimensional space directly in the round. Also, by functioning to help understand complex visual relationships, the model outperforms drawings. This ability is endorsed by a test conducted at Oxford Brookes University that, in comparing the spatial prowess of drawing with modelling, demonstrated that visualising with models completely outstripped the illusory and spatially descriptive powers of graphics. In the test, groups of designer subjects were initially set the task of translating (without representational aids) ten verbally instructed steps in the dissection of a cube. Each step described an increasingly more complex cut, necessitating the mental retention and continued turning of the impression in the mind's eye. At the point when unaided visualisation broke down, subjects were given a pencil and paper and, again, when this was found inadequate, they were handed a block of Plasticine and a knife. Meanwhile, a second test directly compared the strike-rate between unaided and exclusively graphic and modelled sequences.

The findings demonstrated that both graphical and physical models had overtaken the progress of an unaided visualisation. However, in all cases, use of a three-dimensional model enabled subjects to complete the entire sequence quickly and correctly. The conclusion speculated that, if graphic techniques are the sole method employed in design, alternative solutions which might exist beyond their capacity could remain hidden or even ignored. This supposition is further underscored by countless design tutors who observe the greater spontenous diversity, speed and penetration of student design thinking when working in model form. For instance, to paraphrase the artist-architect Harold Linton: 'As the third dimension involves an expanse of physical depth, architects must consider numerous visual relationships when planning any three-dimensional construction. Scale models are developed so that the different angles of a subject can be envisioned more accurately; models are a useful means of entering and understanding the complex world of visual relationships'. Furthermore, product designer Norman Trudeau has described two design processes. The first is one in which decisons are based on preliminary drawings and sketches which later inform the production of a model. The second begins three-dimensionally; using conceptual maquettes to prototype further models from which drawings later monitor design changes and inform production. Trudeau suggests that the latter approach not only holds the potential for richer rewards but can reinforce a much deeper understanding of the relationship between two and three dimensions.

Architectural models can fulfil a wide variety of roles in both the educational design process and the contemporary practice. Not only can they be used as a means of testing the viability of a spatial configuration or to persuade a client that a proposal is worth pursuing, they can also range from the quickly glued assembly of a few pieces of cardboard to elaborate full-size mock-ups of parts of buildings. Along with drawings of the building, they can be produced as a way of refining judgements, decision-making or conveying information.

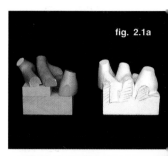

Conceptual models are three-dimensional diagrams fabricated when an idea is still fragile. In their basic form, they can be seen in operation at the dining-table when, in earnest conversation, people spontaneously use condiments and cutlery to illustrate a topographical point under discussion. Similarly, in architectural design, physical diagrams can witness the birth pangs of an idea. By working directly in space, albeit at small-scale, concepts are formed and reshaped as a result of their exploration in three dimensions; a process in which options remain open in design routes; options that might not present themselves to the designer trapped within the confines of paper. They are usually constructed quickly and inventively using found materials or mixed media to symbolise, for example, relationships between the components of a building concept or its rapport with the setting. Used as an initial working design tool by many designers who prefer to test newly forming ideas directly in the space of the idea, the conceptual model represents an intimate and embryonic sketch in three dimensions. However, it is their spontaneity and immediacy that is of great interest because, often being quickly achieved by simple means and in easily worked materials, it is their singular focus on contrast in shape, size, direction, colour and surface treatment, etc., plus their ability to be quickly changed, that make these embryonic design models such a flexible medium. Consequently, conceptual models often encapsulate the essential spirit of a design response and can also capture the all-important first reaction that can sometimes remain as a talisman throughout the ensuing design journey (figs. 2.1a, 2.1b, 2.1c, 2.1d & 2.1e).

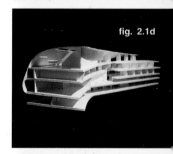

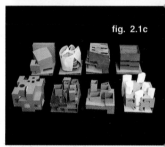

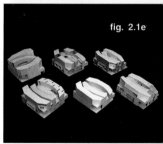

Annette Goderbauer's concept models for Steven Holl's Belleview Art Museum, Washington, and Kiasma Museum of Contemporary Art, Helsinki. © Steven Holl Architects.

For Steven Holl the medium of watercolour painting provides an important and initial conduit for the exploration of his conceptual ideas. Indeed, his daily output of often diminuitive but well-published abstractions witness the birth of a design sequence that, in rejecting any thought of perpetuating an architectural signature style, pursues each new project as a separate and distinct problem. In other words, Holl's approach treats every design scheme as a new beginning; taking into consideration relationship to site, setting, climate and circumstance.

However, the fact that the forms and spaces depicted in Holl's watercolour paintings can become subject to a physical transformation is of great interest. Occurring at a most delicate moment in the life of a design, his sketches and paintings become transmuted into three-dimensional existence - a metamorphosis resulting in some remarkable conceptual models which translate two-dimensional perspective space into a physical presence. This transference is not one that can be replicated by the computer; it results from a rather special 'alchemy' that occurs early in Holl's design sequence. It also exemplifies a special working relationship between one of the most internationally celebrated architects and his modelmaker.

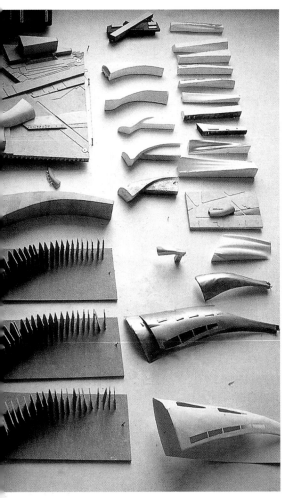

fig. 2.2   Annette Goderbauer's concept model for Steven Holl's Kiasma Museum of Contemporary Art, Helsinki. © Hisao Suzuki.

Built by Annette Goderbauer, the models featured here illustrate Holl's initial concept for the Kiasma Museum of Contemporary Art in Helsinki. The intertwining of the building's mass with the geometry of the city and landscape together with the responsiveness of its shape to significant urban and coastal features is, even at this provisional stage, already well- established (fig. 2.2).

Conceptual models can also occur in retrospect, i.e., as demonstrations of basic formal principles once a design project is completed or when the building is constructed. For instance, Frank Lloyd Wright would publicly and expressively use his hands and fingers to illustrate his architectural philosophy; Oscar Niemeyer will slice into a sphere with a knife in order to explain the geometrical origins of his forms for the Brasilia parliamentary buildings and the Niteroi Museum in Rio de Janeiro, and to demonstrate the unfolding spiral of his Boilerhouse addition to London's Victoria & Albert Museum, Daniel Libeskind will fashion a small expanding paper origami.

Site models are usually built at the outset of designing. They appear as strictly dimensioned representations of the topographic setting for a proposed building design. They record the nature of the site terrain and include evidence of site features that will have impact on the design, such as existing buildings, circulation routes, and planting. Commonly schematically built so as not to detract from the proposed architecture, they tend to be used as a 'base-board' to receive the building design model. Generally speaking, their contours are assembled by glue-laminating layers of sheet material, such as cork, foam-core, plywood, polystryrene, acetates and glass, etc., etc. When constructed early in the design sequence, they function as an important contextual tool when putting an evolving three-dimensional form through its paces (fig. 2.3).

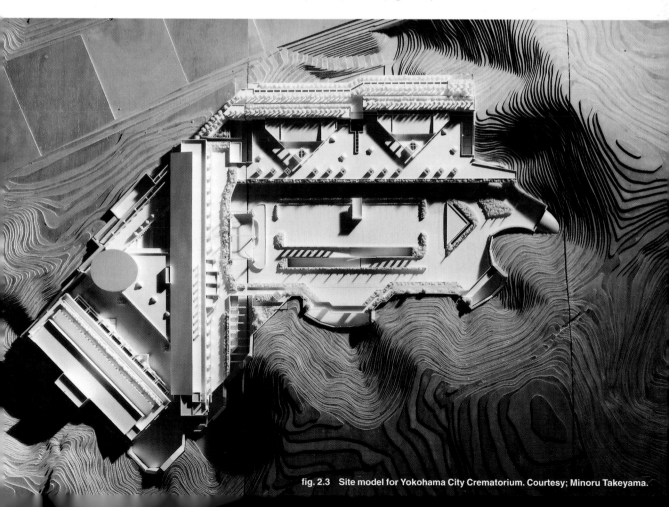

fig. 2.3   Site model for Yokohama City Crematorium. Courtesy; Minoru Takeyama.

Design development models are among the most important and exciting of all the model types. This is because, like their conceptual predecessors from which they are spawned, they are constructed in an unselfconscious manner, their prime aim being to trial the feasibility of a consolidating or challenging architectural form. Consequently, their often spontaneous appearance results from their need to probe the very essence of an architectural concept and, in so doing, often enlist an inventive use of modelmaking media.

By testing the fluidity of a design concept in a more definitive state, they have been described by the late Edmund Happold as 'control mechanisms' that, while referring back to the design objectives, look ahead to possible future opportunities. Happold founded the building engineering consultancy Buro Happold in 1976. Partner in its London office is Michael Cook who strongly believes that too few architects are using models as design development tools. He suggests that there is too much emphasis on the model only to seduce the client. Meanwhile, he and his team are engaged in producing architectural models that are expressly concerned with testing out new ideas. These are not exclusively about structurally-based ideas but often about exploring different shapes, geometries or construction methods that will emerge from experimenting with form and material in different ways - and how these different approaches will ultimately affect the building process. Cook observes that such models are the antithesis of those beautifully crafted versions whose preciousness obviates any real opportunity for easy modification or radical change to test ideas. On the other hand, Buro Happold make literally hundreds of developmental models - each emergent design concept being subjected to successive generations of exploratory maquettes. These are rapidly produced and appear unfinished and crude. They function like quickly made sketches; Once used they get discarded.

The test models encountered in the London model shop of Buro Happold range from trial working models built from traditional materials such as balsa wood, card and soldered wire, etc. to post-conceptual structures assembled from unusual and found materials. These include maquettes with balloons inflated against the retraining ribs of wire, nylon stretched over vacuum formed acrylic moulds, organic forms fashioned from small gauge wire-mesh and even models made using Lego (figs. 2.4a, 2.4b, 2.4c). However, these visually exciting models embody a serious intent as all are real projects commissioned by leading-edge architectural practices, such as Branson Coates Architecture, Foster and Partners and Alsop & Störmer, etc. The models, however crudely built, give expression to ideas and help the design team explore what is possible and communicating new ways of doing things.

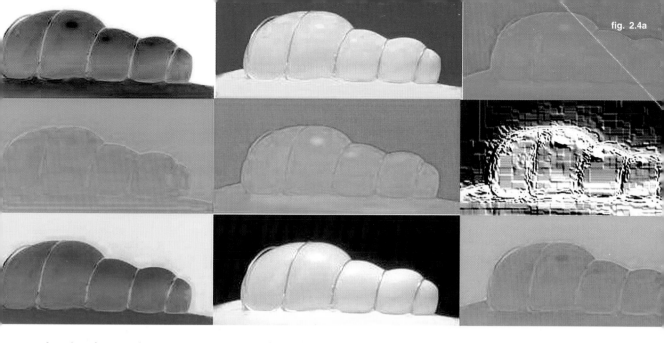

fig. 2.4a

As the form of a new architecture begins to consolidate, a whole series of more specialised building models may be constructed that respond to questions arising from the initial evolution of the architectural form. These are study models, i.e., complete or part models specifically built to address certain issues.

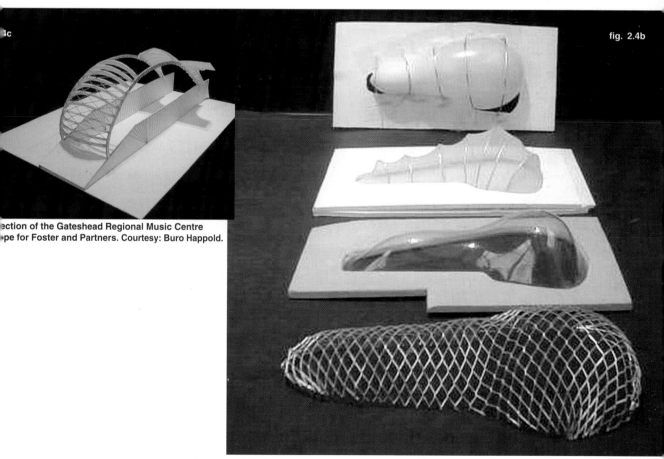

fig. 2.4b

ection of the Gateshead Regional Music Centre
pe for Foster and Partners. Courtesy: Buro Happold.

Development models produced in Buro Happold's modelmaking studio for Alsop & Störmer's proposed night club in Almere, Holland.

Block models represent a whole genre of building study models that, with a purposely restricted palette, carve the external mass of an idea. Favoured by many architects for their reductive expression, they can include a study of urban design implications in relation both to the immediate site-space and to that of surrounding mass. Often built in a single colour and material with any surface detail sacrificed to the abstraction of their pure form, they can also act as three-dimensional bubble-diagrams that, when introduced to the site model, study contextual relationships and activity zones (fig. 2.5).

fig. 2.5   Block study model for Mystic Marinelife Aquarium and Sea Research Foundation. Courtesy: Cesar Pelli & Associates Inc.

Space models represent a popular student maquette that, stageset fashion, is rapidly assembled in simple planes to enclose an individual or continuum of interior space, or to quickly mockup the formation of an exterior facade. Functioning as a kind of planar three-dimensional sketch, space models are often made with no other purpose than to be filmed as walkthrough sequences or photographed - often as an alternative to computer walkthroughs or other simulations (figs. 2.6a, 2.6b, 2.6c).

fig. 2.6a

fig. 2.6b

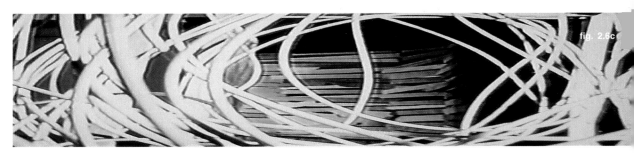

fig. 2.6c

Stills from a model - video animation. John Neale & Basil Kalaitzis.

fig. 2.7a

fig. 2.7b

Structural models function as three-dimensional physical working drawings. Often skeletal in nature they avoid any display of the total external envelope in order to expose, test and demonstrate structural, construction and service systems or their assembly. Made in all scales, structural models are made throughout the design sequence. Like building models, they are sometimes made on the base of a site model because topographic conditions can have a bearing on the manner in which a structure is conceived. They can range from those constructed by the engineer/designer directly to those built by technical modelmakers; they can represent original thoughts, i.e., experimental models that study isolated problems, or exist as fully developed maquettes that communicate a determined structural strategy. In all cases they are an aid to understanding and communication (figs. 2.7a, 2.7b & 2.7c).

'Conceptual-structural models' is a term used by Maurice Jennings and David McKee of Fayetteville, Arkansas to describe the type of models that emanate from their practice. This is the office of the now-retired Fay Jones famous for the delicate wooden tracery of his celebrated Thorncrown Chapel, sited near Eureka Springs. In its current form the office continues the tradition of Jones' church design using a design sequence that quickly moves from sketches into beautifully crafted exploratory models that, in tandem with the planning stage, are built in-house to simultaneously test both structural integrity and building form aesthetic. Jennings and McKee's models are exclusively constructed in linden wood. A close relative of lime, linden is a soft, fine-grain wood traditionally used for the making of sleighs and horse-drawn carriages. Machined into scaled components, linden wood is visually similar to balsa wood and is easy to work, shape and bend. It is used here to explore and text their design at 3/8" scale for the Chapel at Garven Woodland Gardens, Hot Springs, Arkansas (figs. 2.8a, 2.8b & 2.8c).

Structural models for the National Museum of Contemporary Art, Osaka, Japan and for the Mystic Marinelife Aquarium and Sea Research Foundation, Connecticut. Photos: I. Campbell. Courtesy: Cesar Pelli & Associates Inc.

fig. 2.7c

fig. 2.8a

fig. 2.8b

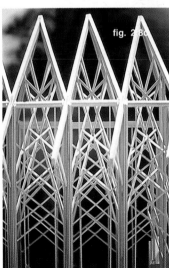

fig. 2.8c

Jenning's and McKee's conceptual structural models for the Chapel of Garven Woodland Gardens, Arkansas. Photos: Maurice Jennings AIA.

fig. 2.9a

fig. 2.9b

Model view of Banking Hall Atrium at scale 1:84, Hong kong Bank Headquarters, Hong Kong (Photo: John Nye) and interior shot of actual atrium (Photo: Ian Lambot). Courtesy: Foster and Partners.

Interior architecture models are built to visualise and address spatial, functional and optical questions and, ultimately, as vehicles to document and demonstrate them to others. In order to provide visual access to their inner workings, building models at different scales are often constructed in 'knock-down' form so that roof planes, exterior wall planes or even complete storeys can be removed. But, when built to larger scales, such as 1:50 and 1:20, interior models can also exist in a much more exciting and specialised role, i.e., as custom-made part-models such as when built as a sectional model. Sectional models three-dimensionally perform like a section drawing, i.e., the slice being formed as a frame - often shown as white - through which internal space is articulated. When wall-mounted and viewed at eye-level, the scale and selectively cutaway nature of such models encourage the viewer to look into rather than at the contained space and, thereby, enable the realisation of an interior architecture in a perceptually more realistic and 'your are there' manner. Like space models, they are also designed to readily receive a camera or camera probe for a photography session aimed at previewing qualities of interior decoration, furnishing and circulation, etc. For example, shown here is a direct comparison between a modelled interior space and a photograph of the same space in actuality. The model was built in-house by Foster and Partners for the client of the Hongkong Bank Headquarters, Hong Kong who, prior to its construction, wanted a prelude of the Banking Hall atrium (figs. 2.9a & 2.9b).

Although not strictly an interior model, a related version is sometimes constructed by interior designers. This is the 'sculptural' assembly of actual samples of the constituent materials, construction connections and colours intended for deployment in an interior space. Although not directly describing the actual spatial configuration, this version of the interior model provides an abstracted assembly of interior design components. Essentially, it is the three-dimensional equivalent of what the architect describes as a 'mood board'.

Lighting models are specialised versions of the interior model. They are built to predict and measure the effect of natural and simulated electric illumination in more light-sensitive spaces such as those in art galleries and museums. In order to aid a more accurate prediction of interior ambience, lighting models often incorporate highly detailed representations of intended colour schemes and surface finish.

Museums and art galleries represent the ultimate light-sensitive environment and we illustrate here two examples of models made to study the impact of light on interior space. The first is yet another interior model made by Foster and Partners to predict the quality of illumination in the glazed lift and first floor lobby of the Sackler Galleries, Royal Academy of Arts, London. Again, to retrospectively judge the efficacy of the shot provided by the scale 1 : 20 model, the view is directly compared with a photograph taken later of the same built space (figs. 2.10a & 2.10b).

Model view of lift and first floor lobby (scale 1:20), Sackler Galleries, London (Photo:Richard Davis) and actual shot of same space showing restored Burlington House facade (Photo: Dennis Gilbert). Courtesy: Foster and Partners.

The second illustration shows two model interiors of galleries in Steven Holl's design for the Belleview Art Museum, Washington. Lighting conditions and a spirit of openness are critical to the unfolding experience of pedestrian movement through the galleries. Underpinning Holl's organisational theme of tripleness are three distinct types of lighting condition correspond to three different gallery spaces on three levels. These are designed in relation to three different concepts of time and three circulation options (fig. 2.11).

fig. 2.11   South Light Gallery, Belleview Art Museum, Washington. © Steven Holl Architects.

Wind tunnel models are built to anticipate any potential deformation of the external envelope or individual construction members of a proposed structure caused by air pressure, suction and turbulence. In order to make visible its pattern of circulation in the test chamber, smoke is introduced to the air source. Apart from studying the negative forces of air pressure on external forms, wind tunnels are also used to study internal ventilation and the efficacy of mechanical service systems.

Presentation models portray the complete and fully-detailed composition of an architectural solution and, usually within evidence of its immediate setting, communicate its finality to others. Not to be confused with the exploratory building model, they take the form of miniature prefigurements of an architecture represented in detail and as a complete entity. Presentation models signal the termination of the design process. Being primarily built for promotion, client consumption and for public relations rather than decision-making, they are less flexible than the rest and are usually intended to convey qualities of external form and its relationships (fig. 2.12).

fig. 2.12   Channel 4 Headquarters presentation model. In-house model built in the Richard Rogers Partnership model shop. Courtesy: Richard Rogers Partnership. Photo: Richard Davis.

There is also a more adventurous form of presentation model that is built specifically for competition submissions and also for exhibition purposes. For example, appearing more like a film set, this model was built by the Richard Rogers Partnership for the 1986 Royal Academy Exhibition (fig. 2.13).

fig. 2.12 Detail of a model made by Tetra shown in the 1986 Royal Academy Exhibition, London. Courtesy: Richard Rogers Partnership. Photo: Richard Davis.

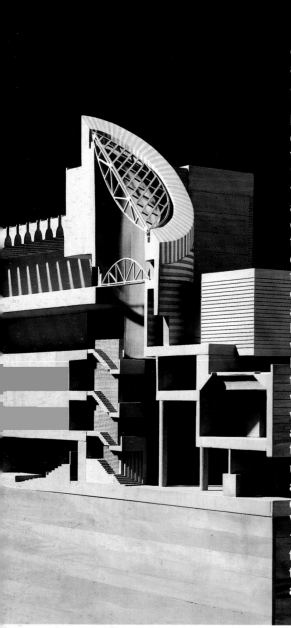

Exhibition models are sometimes built either by or for the architect as a more didactic and analytical version of the presentation model. According to the Ticino-based architect, Mario Botta, this is when 'the poetics and the motives behind the action of the architect are reflectively engaged after a relatively long duration beyond the completion of the building'. He suggests that 'this interval of time can often reveal certain values and limitations'. Botta acknowledges that, although a building cannot be reduced to a mere object, models, when exhibited, can help others to interpret the architectural intent. Their public exposure can function as a 'kind of medium, or filter' which may prompt the viewer to visit the edifice itself. Botta refers to the 1997 exhibition of a collection of his public buildings represented by retrospective sketches, photographs and wooden models mounted in the Palazzo Reale, Naples. Botta's exhibition models become objects that assume their own expressive functions. He writes: 'While they are religiously faithful to the work they represent, they interpret, with their cuts and their sections, the geometry of the spaces of the work. They become autonomous sculptures that guide the visitor through the work of architecture itself'. Botta's models are beautifully crafted in pear wood by Roberto and Stefano Vismara and Simone Salvade to scales between 1:50 and 1:100. He describes the 'subtle variety of their velvety surface' and their miraculous ability to 'evoke the images and the emotions of the architecture' (figs. 2.14a & 2.14b).

fig. 2.14b

San Francisco Museum of Modern Art in pear wood to a scale of 1:100 and Church of Saint John the Baptist, Ticino, Switzerland. Photo: Marco D'Anna. © Mario Botta.

City models are specialised site models that, Lilliput fashion, represent entire urban conurbations. Most major cities have been miniaturised as small-scale models for use by planners, architects and developers. There is the 1:300 model by Unit Twenty Two Modelmakers built in urethene resin and recording everything from Hyde Park to the Tower of London, and also the model of the City of London's financial district. Built by Pipers Model Makers to a scale of 1 : 500 the latter is made from wood and colour coded - each hue signifying one of three stages in the history of the City's growth. However, illustrated here is Fosters and Partners 1 : 1250 scale model of their King's Cross rail terminal master plan shown in its central London setting (fig. 2.15).

fig. 2.15 King's Cross rail terminal master plan. Courtesy: Foster and Partners.

Full-sized prototypes represent an ongoing design debate conducted at full scale. They can range from the 1:1 prefabrication of a structural building component to the full-sized, trial assembly of a room or a portion of a building. Mock-ups are often used to study and refine important elements before final contract drawings are prepared. However, the fine line between a full-sized mock-up and the actual building is crossed when part of a building is erected in its intended materials. This is a comparatively rare undertaking reserved for major projects when a complete specimen storey is erected for testing purposes, such as the study of lighting, acoustics and fire resistance, etc. For example, one such mock-up built in 1995 saw the prebrication of an actual full-scale section of the glass and steel roof structure of Nicholas Grimshaw & Partners Waterloo International Terminal - pre-assembled for testing its accessibility for maintenance (fig. 2.16).

fig. 2.16   **Full-scale mockup for Nicholas Grimshaw & Partner's Waterloo International. Photo: Anthony Oliver.**

Sony Centre, Berlin, block model at scale 1:1000 and styrene models at scales of 1:500 and 1:200 respectively of the building complex and its atrium. Courtesy: Murphy/Jahn.

Following the eighteenth-century example of a full-sized rehearsal in painted canvas of Soufflot's Parisian church, the prototype can also extend to the erection of a mock-up of a complete building. For example, there is the full-scale on-site mock-up in wood and canvas by Mies van der Rohe of his Kröller House prefabricated in 1912 in The Hague, and Lutyens' exploratory prefabrication of timber falsework to study at full scale the 'Spartan romanticism' of his extensions to Castle Drogo in Devon. And then there is the approach of Luigi Nervi in which his building, like a full-scale model of itself, remained susceptible to alteration. His organic concrete forms maintained a 'plasticity' until their completion, sometimes being subjected to a medieval-like modification during the course of their construction.

The journey of a building design can draw from many of the model types outlined above. Indeed, an abridged narrative of the design route can be illustrated using the range of models which function as catalysts to all the other investigative activities of the design process. The project is designed by the Chicago-based practice of Murphy/Jahn architects for their competition-winning design for the Sony Centre in Berlin. Beyond design origination represented by conceptual models comes a block model of the original design; in this case the first definitive and contextual model of the emerging design built in wood to a scale of 1:1000. Reviewed by the architects in conjunction with its Berlin site, the block model functions as a three-dimensional check on initial decisions and also to assess the urban design strategy in relationships of mass, public and private space, effects of daylighting, etc. Once these basic spatio-formal questions have been resolved, a white Styrene 1:500 scale model of the of the proposed Centre was made together with a 1:200 scale model of its Forum; the former being entered for and, indeed, playing its part in winning the international competition (figs. 2.17a, 2.17b & 2.17c).

Following success in the competition, design refinement continued in the form of a series of study models. First came a 1:200 study model built in metal and chipboard, and then a 1:500 scale white-painted wood, Styrene and Plexiglas model which take the complex into a new level of design detailing (figs. 2.18a & 2.18b). An even more highly detailed 1:200 Plexiglas model was then built of the final solution. This model includes colour, street furniture and graphics, etc. and is photographed to simulate the experience of its interior and urban space at ground level and, of course, make judgements about its refinement (fig. 2.19). While the earlier models were made in-house, i.e., in the Murphy/Jahn model shop, this latter model also functioned as the client presentation model and was built by the professional modelmakers, Model Options in Chicago.

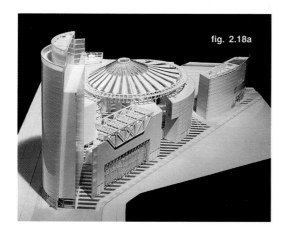

Two in-house study models: one to a scale of 1:200 and the other to a scale of 1:500. Sony Centre, Berlin. Courtesy: Helmut/Jahn.

Presentation model built to a scale of 1:200 by Model Options, Sony Centre, Berlin. Courtesy: Helmut/Jahn.

Even though the form of the Sony Centre was now determined, further decisions came to fine-tune design detailing at the tactile level. These caused scale to increase again, this time in the form of part models made in Plexiglas, metal and wood and assembled at a scale of 1:10 to study detailing and to simulate an eye-level preview of the interior design of the Lobby and, at 1:40 to check at close range the detailing of facade components (figs. 2.20a & 2.20b).

 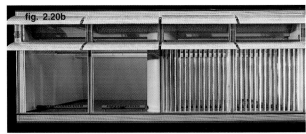

Study models at scale of 1:10 and scale 1:40 investigating lobby details, Sony Centre, Berlin. Courtesy: Helmut/Jahn.

Each model signposts an important moment in the process of design and, as scale increases along the design journey, the form becomes more tangible and more detailed, allowing further investigation into more specialised design issues. This increase in scale also takes the designer ever closer to a multi-sensory experience of the building proposal, until he or she can almost touch the materiality of the unbuilt building. Although the use of models will vary from practice to practice, this gallery of models provides an overview of the role of models that occur within the wider investigative activities of a major international design office.

However, although the materials used in model-making will invariably be different from those used in the later reality they can provide the designer with the tactile experience of shaping physical space. Nevertheless, a model-making fabric can influence the quality of the architecture it replicates. For instance, critics have historically blamed the proliferation of a severe Brutalist and bush-hammered concrete architecture of the fifties and sixties on the widespread use of balsa wood for modelling; others censure those weaned on a Modernist tradition who, relying on the pristine abstraction of white, cardboard models, had helped to spread the 'International Style' anonymity of a raw concrete built environment stripped of ornamentation. Another such relationship between medium and formal resolution is exemplified in the pre-digitial age of automobile design. For instance, the considerable skill in plaster-modelled prototypes developed by Italian designers had produced cars with sharp, crisp edges; while in the United States 'American Wax' and styling clay was used that created designs with softer, more rounded edges. British designers, on the other hand, traditionally had employed timber prototypes which achieved a finish reflecting something of a compromise between the two.

The implied relationship between a model-making medium and the reality of its full-sized outcome questions the use of materials. These will vary from practice to practice as, indeed, they will also vary in relation to the point of occurrence in the process of design. For instance, very different effects are achieved by the computer-milled acrylic models of Ademir Volic for Zaha Hadid Architects (see pages 90-91), the zinc-plated models of Daniel Libeskind (fig. 2.21) . . .

fig. 2.21   'Realistic' zinc-plated study model at scale 1:200, Jewish Museum, Berlin. Photo: Steven Gerrard/Studio Libeskind.

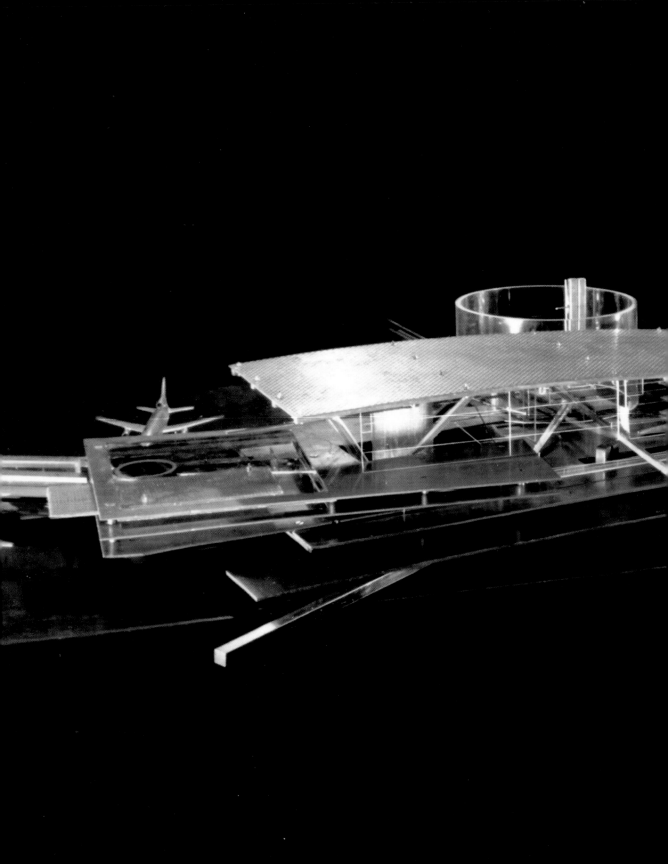

. . . and that for the competition entry by the Office of David Elliot Leibowitz and Ellerbe Beckett for the consolidated terminal for American and Northeast Airlines at New York's JFK Airport. Built under the supervision of Peter Pran, Carlos Zapat and Albert Hennings, this widely published model, while capturing the essence of an architectural idea apparently still in a state of flux, describes the building form in terms of its fragmented, planar aspects using perforated metals and acrylic sheet that represent those used in flight. This model does not represent the design in detail; rather, it depicts the overall form and arrangement of elements but, most important, it demonstrates how materials might be used when pushed to their physical limits (fig. 2.22).

fig. 2.22 Competition entry model for the consolidated terminal for American and Northeastern Airlines, JFK Airport, New York. Courtesy: David Elliot Leibowitz and Ellerbe Beckett.

As we have seen models are made in a wide variety of scale, material and degree of detail and finish; some witness the birth of an architectural notion while others study and consolidate the developing idea. Using different techniques, models are made for many purposes, such as these trial sand castings for Nicholas Grimshaw & Partners International Terminal, Waterloo (fig. 2.23). But how do architects at large approach models and deploy them in the 'journey' of design? To discover this we next turn to three case studies that trace the function of the model in a trio of quite different projects.

fig. 2.23 Component sand castings for Nicholas Grimshaw & Partners International Terminal, Waterloo. Photo: Peter Strobel.

3

Models In Practice

'The use of models in design can flush
out issues that sometimes can be
difficult to visualise; they push
the process forward.'
Martin Marckrow, John McAslan + Partners

In her book, *The Art of the Architectural Model,* Akiko Busch writes that models provide the most efficient means of translating ideas and articulating precise spatial information about notional three-dimensional form. Indeed, architectural models induce an intellectual proximity. This 'nearness' to a concept, she suggests, may derive from childhood associations and, quoting Josephine Gear, '. . . the sense of secretiveness or of sharing private visions that smallness engenders.' She continues: 'If architecture is ultimately and inevitably a public statement, then the architectural model is a preliminary and more intimate dialogue with the facts of building'.

As we have seen, in order to engage in a more 'intimate dialogue with the facts of building' architects will enlist varying model types to problem-solve quite different design issues. But what value do architects place on models, and when and how are they used in relation to other forms of visualisation in the heat of a design process? To find out we trace their occurrence and application in three exciting and quite different projects that emanate from a trio of top architectural practices. We begin with an architect who, using an entrée to the design process similar to that of Steven Holl, employs the medium of painting as a means of initially externalising his ideas.

fig. 3.1   One of Will Alsop's initial 'notional' paintings. © Roderick Coyne.

c/PLEX. Alsop & Störmer

Alsop and Stormer is one of today's leading European practices, with many important projects under its belt, including the Visitor Centre and Control Building for the Cardiff Bay Barrage, the competition-winning design for the prestigious Hôtel du Département in Marseilles, the Peckham Library in London and, also in London, the new Undergound Station at Greenwich North.

What is unusual about William Alsop is his approach to architectural design. His technique derives not from the conventional paper trail of orthographics, but from an initial investigation of ideas expressed in the form of paintings. This essentially private process, sometimes involving up to 30 or so paintings, begins with small abstract experiments worked in a sketchbook using watercolour, ink or acrylic paint. These early paintings explore the spirit of new design ideas in terms of its form, shape and colour. Then once the concept begins to formulate, it can be developed on a larger scale, the size sometimes assuming huge proprtions as the idea begins to consolidate. Alsop has always been deeply interested in painting and has worked in this way for many years; the majority of his earlier projects were solely represented by a painted form. Compared with the restriction of traditionally drafted line drawings, he finds the process a liberation. It provides him with a critical flow of exploratory thoughts and images, free from any preoccupation with detail. In contrast with the work of other painter-architects, Alsop's canvases appear more abstract in their intent and more painterly in their execution. Indeed, much of his exciting and innovative architecture finds its origins in the fluency of his paintwork. But within the sweeps of paint, the enigmatic geometry of his forms and the obvious celebration of colour, lie the seeds of an emerging architecture which, once established on canvas, then moves into an ensuing stage in the design journey, i.e., one that sees its immersion in three dimensions.

We can trace this dimensional transformation in the continuing design process of the competition-winning c/PLEX project - conducted under the leadership of Director, Stephen Pimbley. The concept of c/PLEX is the provision of a new Community Arts and Life Long Learning Centre in Sandwell, West Bromwich for the award-winning Jubilee Arts outreach programme directed by Sylvia King and David Patten. Essentially, c/PLEX is an interactive building with emphasis on invention and discovery; it represents a journey in which visitors will experience various skills, participate in multisensory events and directly engage with artists and their ideas and work.

Alsop & Störmer's project for c/PLEX was initially presented - in competition with other leading practices - as a series of strategies about how they would engage with the client. After their appointment to the project, Alsop produced 10 or so paintings created not to propose architectural intent, but as 'strategic notions' to stimulate a debate with the clients about the possibilities of the project (fig. 3.1, see page 48). Then followed a series of client workshops in which early concepts were developed and presented as 'sacrificial ideas', i.e., ideas which could be interrogated by the clients and also directly engage them in the decision-making procedure. During these workshops both designers and clients exchanged sketched ideas; this graphic dialogue progressing to more definitive ideas and the development of a basic formal strategy (fig. 3.2). Pimbley describes this close client collaboration as an interesting design tool. It was not only an immensely enjoyable experience for the clients but, through an ensuing and continuing engagement, was one that would make them valued members of the design team. The result of this initial design phase later came to be summarised in a single perspective image (fig, 3.3). This already identified the main configuration of the building, i.e., an extruded skybox accessed by a funicular and elevated above a public square.

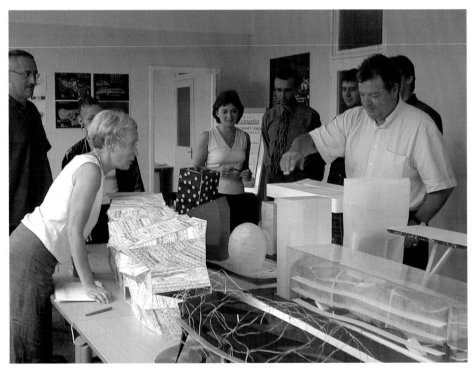

fig. 3.2 Design team-client workshop. © Roderick Coyne.

fig. 3.3 Computer-modelled visualisation. © Roderick Coyne.

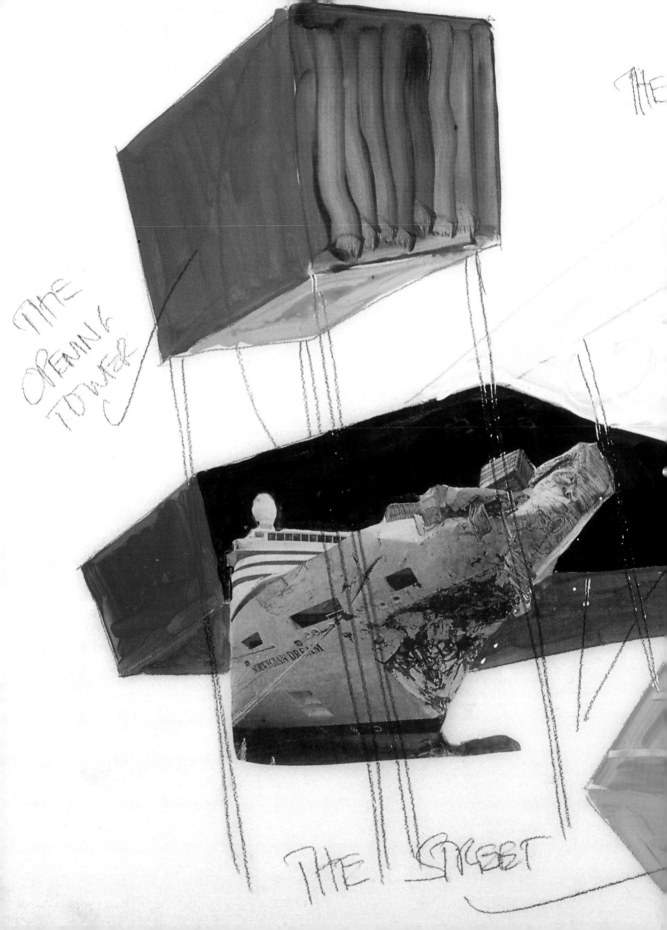

THE OPENING TOWER

THE STREET

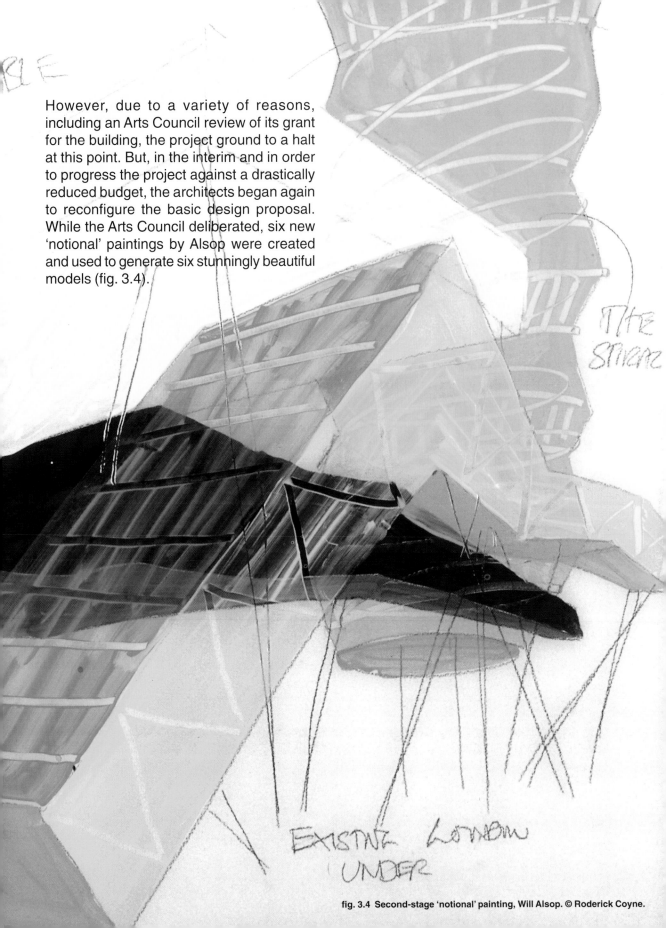

However, due to a variety of reasons, including an Arts Council review of its grant for the building, the project ground to a halt at this point. But, in the interim and in order to progress the project against a drastically reduced budget, the architects began again to reconfigure the basic design proposal. While the Arts Council deliberated, six new 'notional' paintings by Alsop were created and used to generate six stunningly beautiful models (fig. 3.4).

fig. 3.4 Second-stage 'notional' painting, Will Alsop. © Roderick Coyne

The models were not meant to copy the content of Alsop's paintings nor to replicate any apparent physical size, shape or mass. Rather, the models were built to 're-engineer' the original conversation about design possibilities. However, it is this particular sequence of models, some of which are illustrated here (and others on pages 126-129), which are of interest because they are spontaneously constructed in paper by architecture students who frequently work in the practice and, under the guidance of Pimbley, were assigned the task of capturing in three dimensions the spirit of the paintings (figs. 3.5a & 3.5b). These represent the quintessential supermodel, i.e., design development models that exhibit all the spatial qualities of mass, tactility, colour and, above all, vitality. It is their immediacy and spontaneity that capture the essence of the idea and take us to the very heart of a design concept! Indeed, as Pimbley explains: 'It was through these models that we found the solution that now drives the scheme'.

fig. 3.5a

fig. 3.5b

Conceptual models derived from paintings. © Roderick Coyne.

fig. 3.6 c/PLEX model built to a scale of 1:200 by Unit 22.
© Roderick Coyne.

fig. 3.7 c/PLEX model built to a scale of 1:200 by A Models.
© Roderick Coyne.

fig. 3.8 c/PLEX computer model superimposed on site. © Roderick Coyne.

The models were later submitted for scrutiny and reaction to the wider West Bromwich community together with participating artists in the Community Arts programme and, of course, the clients. Feedback that recognised workable ideas exhibited within and across the six models was then distilled into a single, second-stage model professionally built to a scale of 1 : 200 (fig. 3.6). This took on board all the various ideas as well as addressing client specification in terms of areas, accessibility, budget, etc. to make an iterative leap forward.

A succession of models followed, each re-engaging the clients and each fine-tuning the design of the last. During this phase the architectural form coalesced into the configuration shown in this coloured styrene, acetate and card model which, after 14 months of project involvement, was constructed by A Models to momentarily fix the idea in time (fig. 3.7). Here we see the formal arrangement of the building consolidating into its overhead 'surreal street of shops' (now accessed by visitors by an internal elevator) and its unwinding ramped 'underworld' comprising audio-visual pod, interactive events, experiences and exhibits (fig. 3.8). Meanwhile, the building is also seen as open to interpretation by in-house artists who can opportunistically use its voids, spaces and surfaces as a 'canvas' for their work. Indeed, even the external envelope is conceived as a potential support for artwork because artists will be encouraged to cumulatively add their work to its structure; thereby, providing an ever-changing elevation that will additively grow and be marked both by the passage of time and the impulse of creativity.

Pimbley regards the model as a crucial ingredient in the design process: 'There has been such a positive engagement with the client at all stages, we have been talking to them about modifications and changes almost on a weekly basis. More often than not we use the model to describe those changes' (fig. 3.9).

Against the background of a practice that experiments with more adventurous techniques of visualisation, Pimbley concludes: 'The ambition is always that the initial (and sometimes a sacrificial notion) is realised unfiltered into a form that will engage design dialogue as early as possible. This is a liberating approach to the making of architecture; it is opposed to the idea of draughtsmanship and of finely detailed architectural models. It facilitates a freedom both for the client and design team to avoid the predetermined and to range free and explore. It is a way of dreaming the essence of the project'.

fig. 3.9 c/PLEX model built to a scale of 1:200 by A Models. © Roderick Coyne.

The Eden Project. Nicholas Grimshaw & Partners

The Eden Project will be a showcase for global biodiversity. Its main theme is the story of man's dependence on plants. It comprises two enormous climatic enclosures known as biomes. The largest enclosure houses the humid tropics clime containing plants from rainforest-type regions such as Amazonia, West Africa, Oceania and Malaysia, etc. The second enclosure houses a warm temperate clime, such as that found in the Mediterranean, California and the South African Cape. Outside the controlled environments of the biomes are ancillary buildings, such as a Visitor Centre, that will utilise earth construction techniques. The site occupies around 50 hectares of landscaped grounds centred on a disused China clay quarry in St. Austell, Cornwall which, enjoying a relatively mild climate, will allow important species of non-indigenous plants to be grown and showcased.

Already well-established as one of Europe's leading architectural practices, Nicholas Grimshaw & Partners were appointed to the project back in 1995 on the strength of their high profile Waterloo International Terminal in London (see page 39). One of the project architects, Michael Pawlyn, describes an initial design phase ending with a 1 : 200 scale model built by Andrew Ingham & Associates that represents an adaption for this project of the structural enclosure system already rehearsed by them on the Waterloo Terminal building (fig. 3.10). However, prior to the making of this model the site had changed from one in the 'Cornish Alps', i.e., the slopes of China clay spoil, to the present quarry site at St. Austell. It was the existence of this model that highlighted the difficulty of applying a rather deterministic form to a site not only irregular in topography but, because the quarry was still active at this time, one where levels were constantly changing! While the initial design proposal provided a powerful image for what was to prove for the clients a protracted period of fund-raising, the design team used the interim for an extensive and rigorous re-evaluation of their proposal and a re-addressing of the design 'opportunity' presented by a continuously changing terrain.

fig. 3.10 First phase Eden Project model built by Andrew Ingham & Associates. © Michael Dyer

The next design phase involved computer modelling. During this period, project associate, David Kirkland, came up with the idea of intersecting spheres. Experiments followed with computer-modelled three-dimensional geodesic geometries, various arrangements o f intersected spheres being strung together and set into a 3D model of the terrain. This exhaustive study led to the application of the geometry in a second physical model, this time CNC (Computer Numerically Controlled) milled in timber and brass by The Network to a scale of 1 : 200 (fig. 3.11).

fig 3.11 Second-stage model by The Network. © Michael Dyer

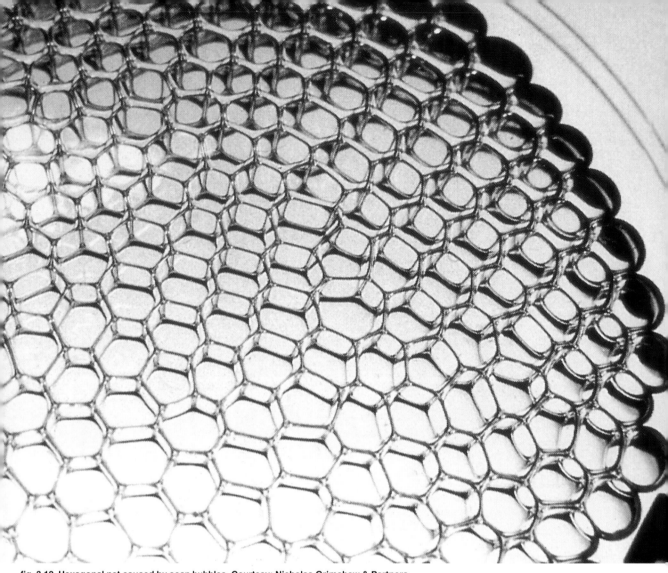

fig. 3.12 Hexagonal net caused by soap bubbles. Courtesy: Nicholas Grimshaw & Partners.

Meanwhile, and in order to resolve geometrical problems both between the 'meshing' of the net of spheres to each other and, most important, at the points at which they touch the undulating ground, the architects investigated different three-dimensional net configurations and junctions. To do so, they used varying clusters of hexagons and pentagons in which the polygonal planes in the geodesic grid changed in size in relation to the size of the sphere. Pawlyn explains that to inform this stage they studied many examples from nature - hexagons appearing widely as an efficient principle of structural integrity in, for example, dragonfly wings and soap bubbles (fig. 3.12).

However, a critical observation was the fact that when the grid met a primary structural element, it distorted - the size of the hexagons modifying to join at right-angles. This information was passed to the model maker in the form of 3D computer files. He was asked to replicate this natural geometrical distortion and experiment with joining the hexagons at right-angles. Although this didn't quite work out, the physical model did provide valuable information on the edge condition, Pawlyn explains: 'It is so much easier than the computer to visualise what is happening. One of the difficulties with geodesic spheres is the understanding of the varying grain of hexagons and pentagons - especially where they intersect with the ground'. A further consideration was the retention of a flat plane on each of the constituent polygons. This was interrogated using a hands-on exploration conducted with a soldered copper wire model (fig. 3.13). Pawlyn describes that, although some aspects of the design could be accomplished on the computer, others became clearer as physical models helped to resolve some questions raised in the process.

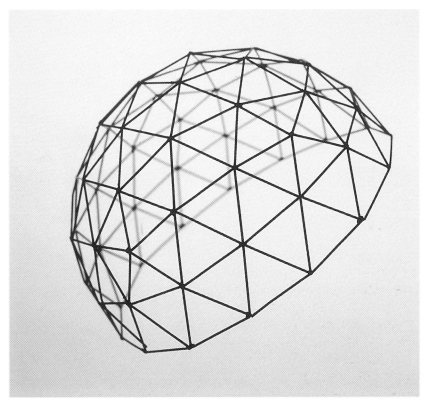

fig. 3.13 Exploratory copper wire model. © Michael Dyer.

Albeit the model made by The Network came close to visualising the project, the main change since its construction was the shift from a single-layer geodesic structure to one incorporating a double-layer steel space-frame. Called a 'Hex-tri-hex system', this comprises an outer skin of hexagons and an inner layer composed of hexagons and triangles - the two connected by diagonals. This system came to dramatically reduce the weight of the steel. The space-frame is enclosed with transparent, inflated foil ETFE (ethyl tetra fluoro ethylene) pillows comprising three layers of polymer material - the complete structure giving 'an impression of a biomorphic organism'. Mock-ups of the ETFE pillows were later prototyped to full-scale in Bremen, Germany for testing purposes together with one whole hexagon frame complete with its inner structure (fig. 3.14).

Finally, Pawlyn acknowledges the debt to the Buckminster Fuller concept of making a one-kilometre diametre geodesic sphere that could be enclosed in a lightweight material and, with a buoyancy resulting from a very slight temperature difference between inside and outside, be light enough to float on air. 'At that time, Fuller didn't have the material', says Pawlyn, ' . . . but I think that EFTE is that material. This scheme reflects Fuller's dream in that we can produce an extremely lightweight sphere'. Indeed, Pawlyn has calculated that the weight of the space-frame is equal to that of the volume of air it encloses!

Although this intensive design process was mainly computer modelled, it was the incidence of physical models and prototypes that, by landmarking important design moments en route, provided impetus to the project. By verifying each stage, the physical models provided a watershed which not only progressed this ground-breaking project, but helped push structural ingenuity into a new state-of-the-art (fig. 3.15).

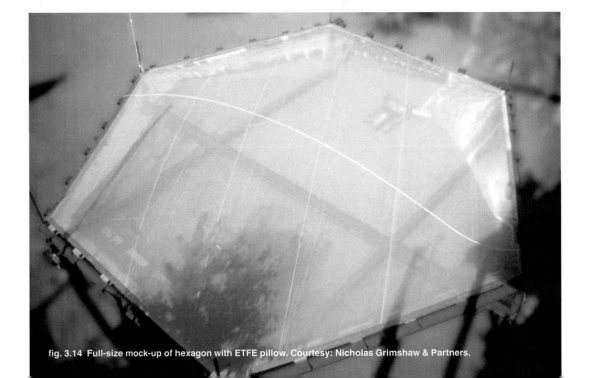

fig. 3.14 Full-size mock-up of hexagon with ETFE pillow. Courtesy: Nicholas Grimshaw & Partners.

fig. 3.15 The Eden Project on-site. © Simon Dolling.

Queen Victoria Street (Salvation Army Headquarters). John McAslan + Partners

John McAslan + Partners stands out among the newer British architectural practices for its inventiveness, versatility and commitment ot the art of architecture. Apart from having built in Europe, Japan and the USA, as well as Britain, McAslan's concern for history has led his studio into rehabilitation and adaptive projects for classic Modernist icons. For example, there is their refurbishing of Erich Mendelsohn's and Serge Chermayeff's De La Warr Pavilion in Bexhill, Surrey (1936) and the remodelling of Frank Lloyd Wright's Florida Southern College in Lakeland, USA (1938-58). However, across their highly articulate and impressive body of new and restorative work is a central concern: insistence on an appropriate use of materials and a creative use of space and form. It is a concern that sees the model playing a crucial role in their design process.

A Director of the firm is Martin Markcrow. He describes two strands in their use of models: as design development maquettes and as client presentation tools. 'Models focus attention on all aspects of the building design - flushing out all those unresolved junctions, elevations or elements that can so easily be skirted or fudged in a drawing. With a model you can't avoid these details. You have to confront them head on'.

Models are continuously used in the practice to push the process on and to quickly address all the design issues that have to be made in order to convey information to a modelmaker. In other words, those outstanding issues which inform the modelmaking process are often the very same issues that inform the actual building. This inter-relationship between modelmaking techniques and building construction stems from Markcrow's student days at the Royal College of Art when he built professional models as a sideline. Finding the experience invaluable, he learned that the way junctions are articulated in the model are often similar to or precisely the same as the way they are articulated in the real building. Consequently, the practice will often build in-house or commission professional models specifically to force these issues into the open.

To illustrate the role of the model in the practice Markcrow describes their function as critical 'stepping-stones' through the design process of their competition-winning proposal for the replacement Salvation Army Headquarters building on a prestigious site just south of St. Paul's Cathedral in London. Models were used from the outset; initial discussions with the clients at the competition stage enlisting small colour coded models built by James Wink which, in direct comparison with a sister model illustrating the inflexibility and inefficiency of the existing building, described the maximum development potential of the site. Built to a scale of 1 : 500 and simply made from thin sheets of colour-sprayed Perspex stacked as detachable floorplates. these are termed 'colour usage models' and are widely used in the practice. 'Clients love them', says Markcrow, ' . . . they are not architectural models as such but they clearly diagrammise the concept and the functional configuration of a building (fig. 3.16).

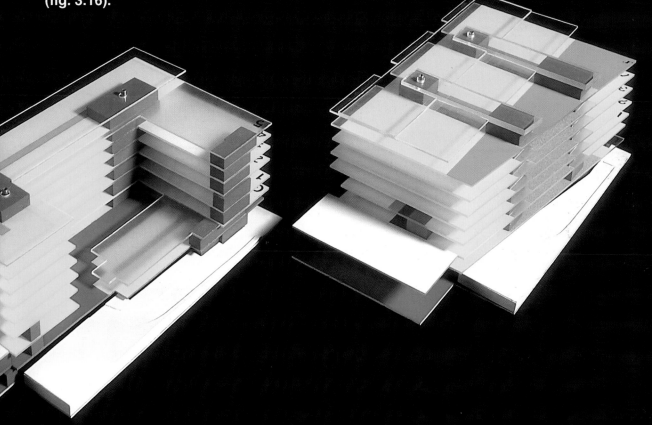

fig. 3.16 James Wink's 'colour usage' models. © Andrew Putler.

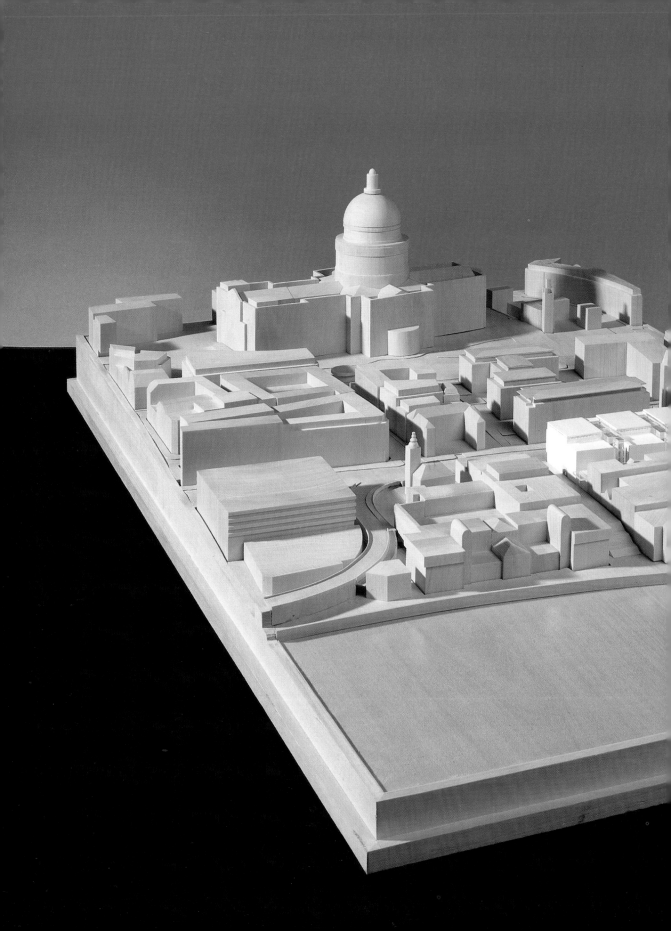

After a second developmental and refining sequence of colour usage zoning maquettes were made, next came two 1 : 500 scale block models: one built in-house by Martin Harris that tested the outline proposal and another professionally built by The Network modelmakers that tested the massing of the quickly evolving form against the sensitivity of its urban setting on a timber site model made by James Wink (fig. 3.17). Indeed, at this stage floorplate configuration and mass were already beginning to consolidate into a recognisable version of the ultimate form.

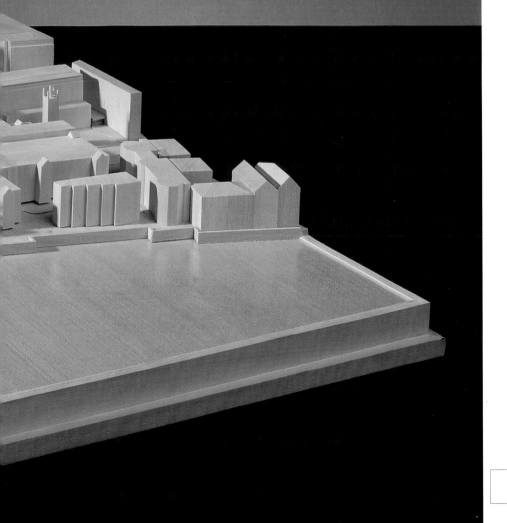

fig. 3.17 Block model by Martin Harris inserted in James Wink's site model. © Andrew Putler.

fig. 3.18 Facade detail study model built to scale 1:25 by Unit 22.
© Andrew Putler.

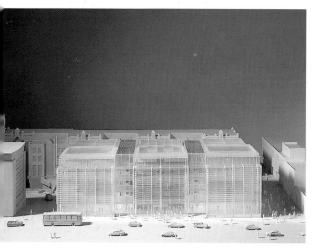

fig. 3.19 Presentation model built to scale 1:200 by James Wink.
© Andrew Putler.

Each of these and ensuing models are, of course, interspersed with intensive periods of designing, but each model appears to consolidate the process and represent a 'marker' for the next design phase. Further 'landmark' models included one built in-house by Martin Harris to examine the proportions of the atria spaces at a scale of 1:50, and another built by Unit 22 modelmakers from Chemiwood, Perspex and acetate to interrogate different facade detail design and cost issues at 1 : 25 scale (fig. 3.18).

Then came a 1: 200 presentation model built by James Wink which was used to assist design development and also for presentation purposes to the statutory bodies (fig. 3.19) Subsequently, a second facade study model was made at 1:50 scale this time by The Network modelmakers (fig. 3.20). Aside from the latter being exhibited in the 1999 Royal Academy Summer Exhibition this, together with Wink's modified presentation model, was successfully submitted to the Corporation of London Planning Committee and the Royal Fine Arts Commission.

fig. 3.20. Facade detail model built to scale 1:50 by The Network. © Andrew Putler.

Given the size of the building project, design time was relatively fast - from competition stage to revisions and planning permissions in eight months. Markcrow explains that this was partly due to the use of models: 'They literally do speed up the process. What is so valuable about them is that they are not only good for client presentations but you can test alternative approaches to either discount or develop them further. Also, models are very important for relaying design intent to the engineers and other consultants involved. Engineers can often misunderstand drawings whereas a model will describe to them exactly what you are seeking to achieve; they provide a design team tool. For instance, on this project we were building in the City of London for the first time and we had to liase with Corporation Planners, the Royal Fine Arts Commission and English Heritage. During such meetings it was critical to present good visual material in order to both clearly communicate design intent and to negotiate the scheme through the statutory process'.

The increasing scale of models used in this design sequence result from a combination of in-house and professionally built versions. When commissioning the latter McAslan + Partners will tend to employ different modelmaking firms at different stages in the design sequence. This, Markcrow explains, is because various modelmaking firms have become identified with different modelmaking skills, techniques and materials and, consequently, different genres of architectural prototype.

In order to explore this relationship and also to examine the contribution of the modelmaker to the design process and, indeed, to those architects with whom some have become identified, we now turn to the study of a selection of those recognised as leading exponents of their craft.

4

The Makers of The Supermodel

'The best modelmakers function as the 'backroom boys' of architectural design; their models often filling the gaps and fleshing out the detail in the space between concept and its physical expression.'

Matthew Wells, Techniker

Hidden behind the reputation of each of the leading international architects is a modelmaker. Whether built in-house or by a freelance modelmaker, the person who constructs their supermodels makes far more than just a passing contribution to the ultimate appearance of the architecture. Working with new techniques and a technology that has dramatically changed over the last few years, and often building from scant information against pressing deadlines, the best of the modern modelmakers are often given a free hand to interpret the design and attempt to extrude the essence of the architect's intentions. In so doing, several of them have, while employing specific materials, palettes and techniques, developed and even created for their patrons the familiar and associated signature design style used in the three-dimensional representation of their buildings. Consequently, a special relationship of trust has developed between some designers and the builders of their models and, although unsung in the architectural press, many are considered as an integral part of the design team.

However, an important issue emerges when models are used to communicate design ideas. In discussing the role of the modelmaker and the presentation impact of architectural ideas, Thomas Fisher, Executive Editor of the now defunct *Progressive Architecture*, describes three illusions in the communication of architectural design. The first illusion refers to the fact that we all suffer from 'the illusion of technique'; the idea that providing we know how to make a model, a correct and meaningful outcome will result. This gives rise to a second illusion. Just as we can delude ourselves into believing that technique is everything so, too, can we make the opposite mistake of assuming that technique means nothing. In other words, that the model itself has no real impact on the ideas being communicated. In referring to the writings of Marshal McLuhan, Fisher suggests that we transgress if we think that a medium is transparent, something that we see through, without distortion, to the message beyond. Meanwhile, he proposes that every presentation medium has inherent limitations and distortions that affect the message. Sometimes the distortions can so dominate the intended meaning that the medium itself becomes the message. In other words, Fisher suggests, 'When we don't take the effects of the medium into account, they will take us'.

The third illusion is based on the premise that, compared with those who create three- and two-dimensional presentations, the originator of a design idea is invariably seen as all-important. In other words, the designers of a project take all the glory, while those who produce the models (and the drawings) are ignored or, even worse, considered uncreative. Fisher concludes that this is a naive view as, just as the medium affects the message so, too, does the modelmaker's viewpoint effect its final communication. He or she is a translator of ideas and translation is anything but a pedestrian activity. It is a subjective process open to a wide range of interpretations that can greatly colour our perception of an idea. Therefore, in translating the intent of the designer, the modelmaker unavoidably injects his or her own view of the design. In so doing, he or she serves as a critic, bringing their own interpretation to the appearance of the design intention and, sometimes, in their choice of materials used in its simulation, adding a new dimension to its expression.

Despite this design contribution, however, a class difference prevails within the architectural profession. A telling example of this inequity (unlike that afforded photographers) is the lack of acknowledgement extended to modelmakers. The fact that the architectural and, indeed, model photographers demand such credit and will watchdog publications in order to ensure that it occurs, does not excuse the lack of recognition afforded to their authors. Therefore, what follows is an examination of the apparent ressurgence of modelmaking and the contributions of both in-house and independant modelmaker in the creative process.

A more widespread interest in the work of professional modelmakers has been fostered by a series of exhibitions which have showcased the virtuoso skills of those who have been described as the 'backroom boys' of architectural design. One such exhibition was housed at the Architectural Association in 1993 and dedicated to the projects of Alsop & Störmer. The centrepiece of the show was an eight-metre long supermodel of their 'Big Blue' City Hall building (Hôtel du Département) for Marseilles. Although no photographs survive, this room-sized model is of interest because its existence resulted from the loss in France of the numerous concept, development and presentation models made in the build-up to its actual construction. However, more interesting is the fact that, rather than merely replicate the actual design, this supermodel used elements from the project to reinterpret the design in a combination of form and materials.

This renewed interest in models was also detected by a journalist reporting on the AJ/Bovis awards in the Royal Academy of Arts Summer Exhibition in 1994 in which design models seems to scoop all the major prizes. In lamenting the demise of the architectural drawing. he wrote: 'a characteristic of this show is the domination of models, model photography and computer graphics, with little in the way of stunning draughtsmanship'. Other influential exhibitions of the time include that for the display of eight pedestrian bridges for London's Docklands in 1994 and later, in 1996, the Living Bridges exhibition. This exhibited ideas from a competition in which an invited group of internationally known architects submitted ideas for a habitable bridge connecting Temple Gardens to the South Bank of the River Thames - an exhibition which climaxed in the acrylic model of joint-winner Zaha Hadid Architects. However, alongside computer models and drawings were physical models reconstructing both speculative and existing habitable bridges from the past.

Fourteen historical 'living bridge' models were built especially for this exhibition by Andrew Ingham & Associates. Each model was displayed spanning a series of tanked watercourses, their unfamiliar juxtaposition demonstrating dramatic scale differences between, say, that of the design for the Ponte Vecchio in Florence and Palladio's proposed design for the site on which the Venetian Rialto Bridge now stands (fig. 4.1).

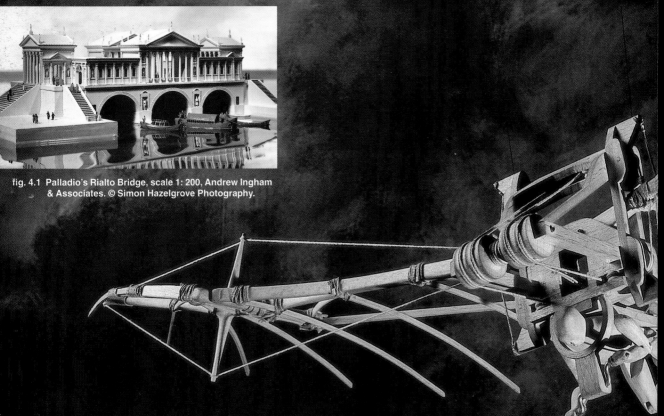

fig. 4.1 Palladio's Rialto Bridge, scale 1: 200, Andrew Ingham & Associates. © Simon Hazelgrove Photography.

Andrew Ingham & Associates

Andrew Ingham & Associates first came into the public eye in 1988 during its former existence as Tetra Associates and the widespread media attention given to its spectacular full-scale mock-up of Leonardo da Vinci's flying machine. Based on research into surviving drawings and manuscripts, this supermodel was reconstructed under the direction of James Wink. With a wingspan of 36 feet and a payload of 650 lbs, the contraption was made from polished beech, iron, brass, coir rope, and leather, Complete with its windlass and pulleys and 'controlled' by a dummy Daedalus harnessed into its undercarriage, the machine was suspended to 'fly' above the display of various reconstructions of Leonardo's ingenious designs in the 1989 exhibition celebrating his powers of invention at the Hayward Gallery (fig. 4.2).

If Andrew Ingham & Associates represents one of the leading freelance modelmaking firms who work for the well-known architects, the designer and the modelmaker in a small practice can often be the one and the same person. Meanwhile, in some of the mega-practices, such as Foster and Partners in London and Frank Gehry in Santa Monica, models can be made in-house where a close working relationship can develop between modelmaker and architect. Such an intimate relationship is illustrated in the exciting models of Chris Barber who runs the small workshop at Terry Farrell & Partners and where he operates as an important member of the architectural design team.

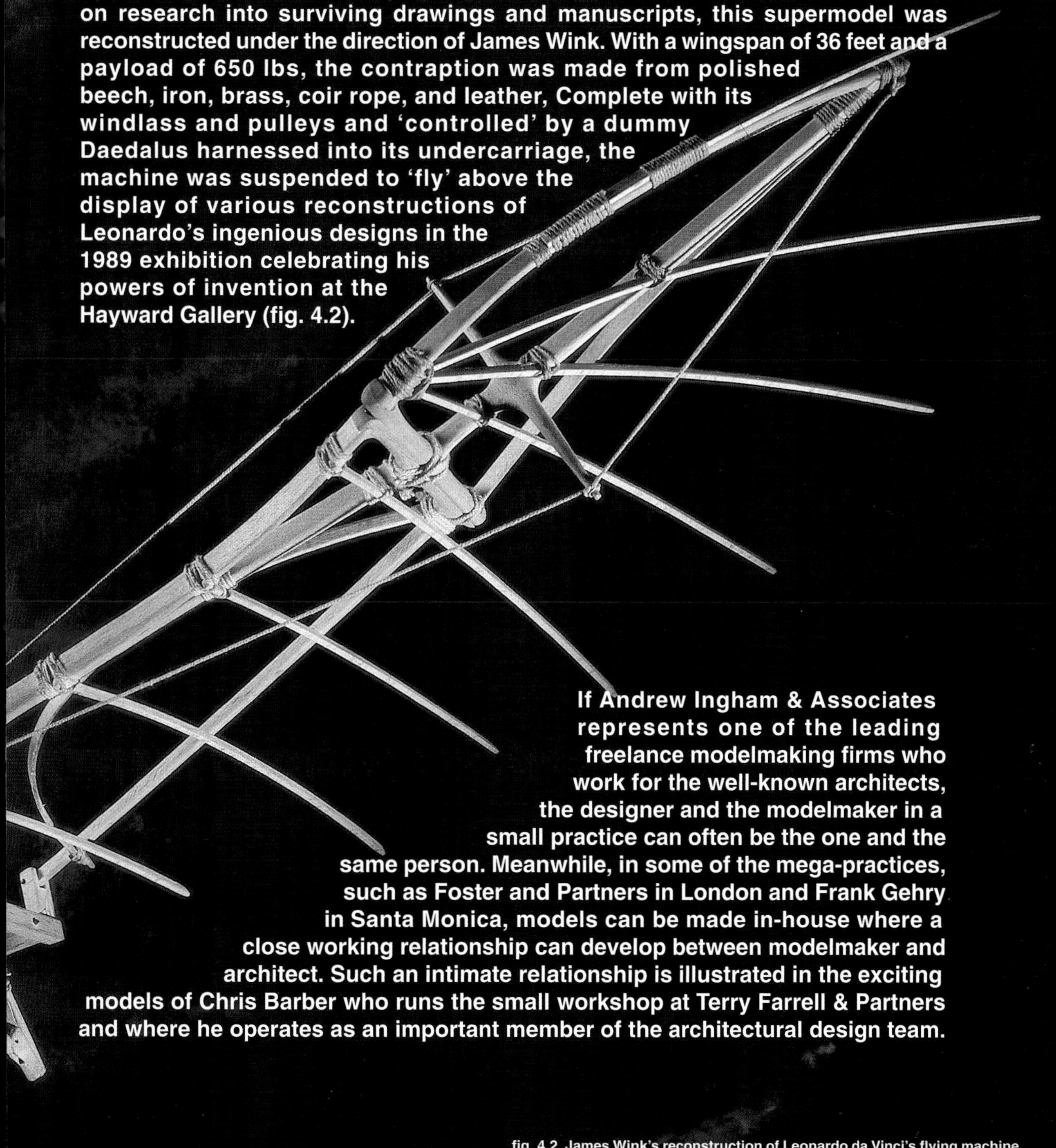

fig. 4.2 James Wink's reconstruction of Leonardo da Vinci's flying machine.

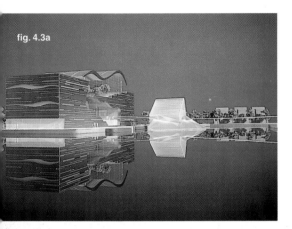

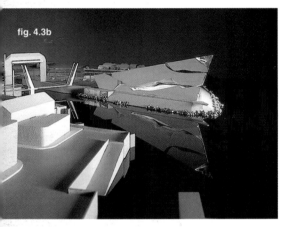

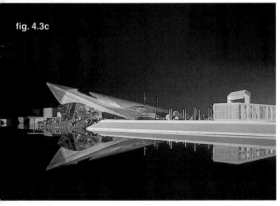

National Aquarium and 'The Deep'. Courtesy: Terry Farrell
& Partners. Photos: © Andrew Putler.

Chris Barber, Terry Farrell & Partners

Working almost exclusively in Styrofoam, Perspex and plastics. Chris Barber's models engage in design development from a very early stage, often worked quickly from scribbled notes and sketched orthographics to give physicality to both exploratory and evolving stages of a new project. Notable among his recent and comparatively small-scale supermodels are two competition-winning aquariums: the widely published National Aquarium sited on a jetty in London's Docklands and 'The Deep' - the latter representing a Millennium-funded Ocean Science Complex to be located in Kingston upon Hull in 2001 at the confluence of the Humber and Hull rivers. Both built to 1:500 scale, Barber's models of these projects have an air of spontaneity and a freedom of expression that is entirely in tune with the creative versatility of their designer - their smallness assuming human scale when photographed. For instance, his development model for the National Aquarium - which provided a key source for its   persuasive presentation imagery - was quickly constructed using photographically printed patterns on nickel plates which were then acid-etched before lamination on to Perspex. More recently, his conceptual model for 'The Deep' is a super-glued assembly of four layered shards of clear Perspex variously sculpted and polished and selectively colour-sprayed with a thin film of blue acrylic cellulose and polycarbonate paint to achieve its required translucent and 'glacial' appearance. Shaped like an enormous mountain of ice, the triangulated and tilted assembly reflects Farrell's architectural metaphor of geological plate tectonics around 250 million years ago when faults caused the earth's crust to buckle and form peaks and depressions (figs. 4.3a, 4.3b & 4.3c).

Cranes a
the Consulate

Barber describes his deep sense of belonging in the design practice; his rapport with Farrell finding him invited into initial design briefing sessions. Here, unencumbered by an architectural education that schools in precedent and possible preconceptions of what a design might be, he remains completely open-minded to Farrell's conceptual ideas - often described in metaphorical terms, such as that for 'The Deep'. Consequently, Barber concludes ,'When Terry says I want the form to be like a water-lily, or like a bird, I feel the freedom to respond directly and instinctively to these three-dimensional ideas'.

fig. 4.5a

The development models produced by Barber for Farrel & Partners competition-winning Great Hall and secondary flight control tower for Korea's new Inchon International airport in Seoul again highlight that special relationship between modelmaker and architect. With shades of George Pal's flying machines in his movie *War of the Worlds*, Farrell's design sits as an enormous sculptural icon at the heart of the Airport masterplan to reflect Korean culture, nature, flight and the future - a concept driven from the outset by his sketched metaphor of a flying crane (fig. 4.4). However, the extremely complex three-dimensional nature of its conceived form proved difficult to visualise in drawings. Therefore, hand-carved in Styrofoam by Barber and working in close collaboration with the project architect, an exhaustive sequence of early conceptual models was produced. Each successive model responded to a further evolutionary phase of Farrell's elegant bird-like form and, being fixed by the co-ordinates of height and its tripod footprint, each version probed alternative design avenues into the potential nature of its formal existence.

fig. 4.5b

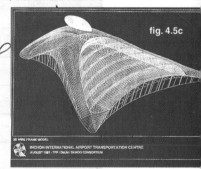

fig. 4.5c

2D WIRE FRAME MODEL
INCHON INTERNATIONAL AIRPORT TRANSPORTATION CENTRE
AUGUST 1997 - TFP / DLM / SAMOO CONSORTIUM

When resolved, the final form still proved impossible to accurately draw - even when sketched into the computer. Consequently, Barber again carved its conclusive form in Styrofoam, but this time the model was meticulously halved and sectionally sliced against a grid. Each newly exposed section was then scanned into the computer to provide the data from which a definitive wire-frame drawing was achieved (figs. 4.5a, 4.5b, 4.5c & 4.5d).

fig. 4.5d

Physical and electronic models of Terry Farrell & Partners Great Hall for Korea's Inchon International Airport. Photos: Nigel Young.

79

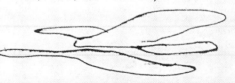

Express 2 or 3 levels
(like a series of elements

Barber's modelmaking at Farrell & Partners is exclusively concerned with giving substance to design ideas. Invariably, these exist as concept and design models which are then used for themselves or via their photographic transformation to communicate with competition judges and clients. However, when destined for exhibition and a public consumption, Farrell & Partners commission modelmaking firms, such as 3DD (Three Dimensional Developments) to construct presentation models (fig. 4.6).

The central role of the working model is endorsed by Terry Farrell who describes his three-stage design sequence as, first, involving draft sketches followed by design development using physical models - the process ending with CAD models. 'This is exactly the process I use. I rely heavily on the physical part. Indeed, of all three mediums I rely much more on the physical model to experiment with shape and form and make design decisions. I primarily work with foam and hot-wire models which are usually quite simple. I particularly like to work with each model having many sub-components, so that a whole range of alternatives can be tried and tested. At the end of the day it is only the eye that can make the real judgement - and the three-dimensional model is the best simulation of the whole thing'. Farrell concludes this this is not a process exclusive to his own practice. On his global travels to international congresses, etc., he is struck by how many leading architects stress the need for developing design solutions using the same process.

fig. 4.6 Final model, Great Hall, Inchon International Airport. Courtesy: Terry Farrell & Partners.

Ademir Volic (Delicatessen)

Ademir Volic is an architect and award-winning designer who trained himself to become a modelmaker. He rejects the idea of being button-holed as focusing on any particular specialism; preferring instead to freely operate across the boundaries of product and furniture design, architecture and manufacturing, etc. After graduating as an architect from Sarajevo before settling in London, Volic first worked in Zaha Hadid's office before going solo in 1994. However, via his modelmaking skills, a rather special chemistry has developed between him and the practice. Indeed, he is responsible for the majority of the prizewinning and widely-published Perspex models associated with Zaha Hadid Architects. He now makes models solely for Hadid because, apart from participating in and feeling a part of the wider creative vision of the practice, he works within an exciting, interactive and extremely challenging design environment.

Volic describes the Hadid design process as a simultaneous series of exhaustive and questioning design 'strands' that, sometimes independently, sometimes interwined, weave a complex of searching design journeys that explore each new project. The strands are represented by chains of different investigative activities: painting, conceptual modelling, drawing and computer visualisation. Involving two and three dimensions and sometimes the dimension of time and movement, these strands represent a voracious design approach incorporating the large and familiar acrylic paintings which explore masterplanning, colour dynamics and texture, a host of cardboard development and study models focusing on context and volumetrics, scaled orthographic drawings that directly address the brief, and computer graphics which probe spatial experience through animated walk-throughs, etc. These multi-dimensional strands ultimately converge but, at key stages en route, they become superimposed and cross-referenced when crucial design decisions are made.

According to Volic, this all-encompassing approach represents an incomparable process; and one capable of transporting us to the boundaries of a unique architectural experience. Moreover, having come to know and understand this process together with its far-reaching implications, he emphasises that this approach is the only way of designing buildings.

Volic is called in to make a model when 'there is something to see'. He will then take away some of the maquettes and drawings and, within a few days, deliver his version of the model. Consequently, in a short space of time - often to meet a looming competition deadline - Volic has first to fully digest the design idea and plan the modelmaking strategy before rapidly and physically translating the given information into a definitive three-dimensional statement. The design process, however, continues well beyond the point of his models. Indeed, they become part of Zaha Hadid's ongoing philosophical debate in which, being concerned with the infinity of space, architecture is discussed in abstraction. Consequently, there is always reluctance to the notion of prematurely 'freezing' a design in some physical reality. Accordingly, 'Zaha literally doesn't want the process to end; the exploration is relentless and regardless of success in a competition. This is when I can be approached for more and more models to be made in different materials. In other words, the journey is not so much about project, but much more about process, and the process is never-ending'.

Volic strongly believes that his contribution to this process is significant, and this gives him a profound, personal satisfaction. He also describes the 'buzz of the dialogue with the architect when deciding upon the ultimate appearance and 'feel' of a model. Sometimes this can reach heated debate when, despite the given specification, he might insist on a particular 'look' as being the best way of communicating the design in model form. For instance, his model for the Concert Hall for the Luxembourg Philharmonic Orchestra was, against some resistance from the practice, built as a white model. Constructed in Perspex, this was the first of Hadid's models to be completely sprayed in white. For this, Volic employed a subtle palette of five different cellulose whites. Using finishes such as 'pearl', matte and different versions of 'silk' finish found in car spray paints, Volic introduced subtle nuances of white through masked subdivisions both across and within the planes of the model (fig. 4.7).

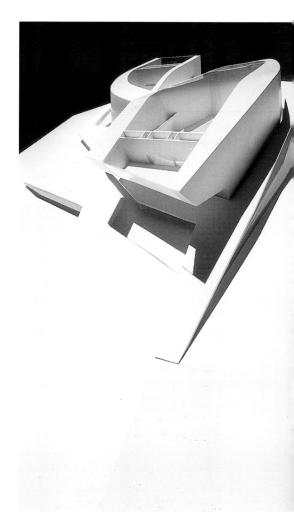

fig. 4.7 Luxumbourg Concert Hall, Zaha Hadid Architects.
Photo: Edward Woodman.

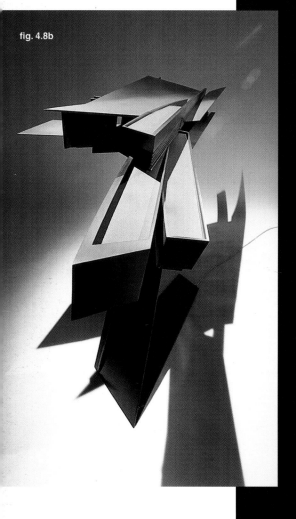

fig. 4.8b

Another unusual model by Volic was his 1: 50 scale mild steel model of the Vitra Museum commissioned from Zaha Hadid by Vienna's MAK (Museum of Modern Art). Weighing 280 kilos and 3 metres in length, the model, at the instruction of the architect, was made to 'fly' above the atrium of the Vitra Museum (figs. 4.8a & 4.8b). Volic fabricated the model using a spot-welded double-skin of mild steel separated by spacer bars. After its welded edges were cleaned and ground, the whole model was sandblasted, its planes then being selectively polished before being stabilised in a spray booth with clear lacquer. The polishing process is of interest because it was used to recreate an effect described by Volic as the 'whoosh', i.e., the dynamic gradation of tone or colour along the trajectory of an architectural plane. In Zaha Hadid's paintings, the 'whoosh' is represented by dramatic colour shifts which, by progressively transforming from one hue to another, further energise the shape dynamic of constituent planes. Meanwhile, this effect in Volic's model is created by the introduction of a graduated light-to-dark finish to the steel that progressively works from highly polished areas to sandblasted and unpolished areas.

fig. 4.8a

Photos: Edward Woodman

fig. 4.9 Clear Perspex model of Zaha Hadid's Cincinnati Centre for Contemporary Arts, Ohio. Photo: Edward Woodman.

Volic's extensive portfolio of models for Zaha Hadid include that for the prizewinning Cincinnati Centre for Contemporary Arts tower in Ohio. This is completely assembled in clear Perspex to provide a superb and totally transparent supermodel - its basement and successive floor plates remaining visible when seen directly from above (fig. 4.9).

fig. 4.10b

Meanwhile, his series of cellulose-sprayed Perspex models for Hadid's Cardiff Opera House not only represent a translucent and beautifully complex architecture but also exemplify a highly complicated modelmaking strategy. For example, in order to programme light into the wall-planes of its five rehearsal rooms, the 3mm thick planes each had to be routed in order to receive miniature runs of LED circuitry - each individual component leaving an exposed contact point. The pre-wired planes of Perspex were then 'plugged' into the model to make a precise connection with mated contact points in its floor slab. This was a kind of 'micro-surgery' that became part of one highly-detailed model built by Volic to a scale of 1 : 200. Augmented by a secondary uplighting system using miniature fluorescents buried beneath the frosted acrylic base, its programmable lighting allows the viewer to control a lighting sequence in which each of the rooms in turn can be illuminated (figs. 4.10a & 4.10b).

fig. 4.10a

Cardiff Bay Opera House, Zaha Hadid Architects. Photos: Edward Woodman.

Another project by Zaha Hadid is described by Jonathan Glancey as being ' . . . a radical critique of existing major art galleries as well as a thing of unexpected beauty'. Glancey refers to the design for the new Centre for Contemporary Arts in Rome which Hadid won against glittering international opposition, such as Steven Holl and Rem Koolhaas. At the heart of a submission including drawings, computer renderings and walkthroughs, etc., was Volic's acrylic model which proved pivotal in the communication of the scheme. Built to a scale of 1 : 500, the model proved to be one of the most difficult modelmaking operations ever attempted by Volic. Indeed, he ranks the project as one of the most sophisticated and complex architectural designs he has ever encountered. It took him three days to figure out how the scheme worked and to plan how the various elements of the model might be achieved. Realising that a piece-by-piece assembly would not achieve the required precision, he turned instead to a CNC (Computer Numerically Controlled) technology and, in order to achieve the intricate tracery of its forms, worked directly from DXF. files of the wireframe plan-forms. These were used to computer-program a small Roland milling machine - the majority of the model's snaking and channelled elements being accomplished in this way. This meant that the complex layering of parallel pathways, each following their spaghetti-like trajectories, and leading in and out of courtyards within the design, were individually and meticulously machine-cut, grooved and polished from 20mm thick

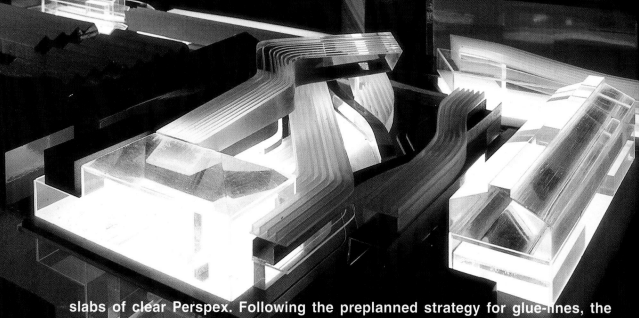

fig. 4.11a

slabs of clear Perspex. Following the preplanned strategy for glue-lines, the components were then carefully and invisibly fused using brush-applied Tensil - a commercial chloroform-based solvent that causes the surface molecules of the acrylic to melt and become fused. Finally, the model was mounted on an opaque and contoured base of Urial - an 'artificial wood' composition sometimes used in prestigious modelmaking projects (figs. 4.11a & 4.11b).

fig. 4.11b

gain we encounter the rather special
elationship that can develop between
he architect and the modelmaker. It is
ne in which each has to independently
perate but, in order to enable the physical
manifestation of the architect's
roposition at such a delicate moment
n its life, both have always to be tuned
nto the same wavelength. What Volic
escribes as the 'buzz' he experiences
manates from his intimate involvement
n the challenging relentlessness of
adid's creative process together with
he electrical charge that is generated
when two dedicated creative forces come
ogether.

Don Shuttleworth: Unit Twenty Two Modelmakers

Apart from setting-up the in-house modelmaking workshop for the Richard Rogers Partnership, Don Shuttleworth over the years has produced models for Nicholas Grimshaw & Partners and Foster and Partners, etc. Since 1989, however, he has made all of the important models for Future Systems. Up until five years or so ago, i.e., before the construction of their first buildings, the model represented the culmination of Jan Kaplicky's and Amanda Levete's design process - the scaled prototype remaining as the only tangible object of the exercise. However, like other 'paper architects' such as Peter Eisenman and Daniel Libeskind, they were to receive their first commissions that would allow them to test their theories in a full-blown architecture.

The first crop of Future Systems structures not only transfers the model into a human-scale reality it also provides an architecture that draws inspiration from the wealth of organic structures found in nature, together with those man-made shapes and forms that have withstood the test of time. It is from such sources that they have evolved an environmental language of form that challenges our Western perceptual conditioning to the right-angle. Indeed, their earlier projects carry names such as 'Peanut', 'Drop' and 'The Wrap' - terms that, in each case, describe the aerodynamic forms of enclosed habitats that have been organically evolved. Realised or not, each project is intensely researched, meticulously detailed and entirely practical and, although not conceived from the well-worn paths of precedent, their practicability and energy efficiency is captured in Shuttleworth's beautifully made models.

Initial communication between Future Systems and Shuttleworth is usually in the form of floorplate delineations and sketches made by Kaplicky of the intended model together with lengthy discussions concerning the ultimate function of the model. Shuttleworth suggests that this transfer process could be directly realised via a computer-milling technology but it is rarely accurate enough at this early stage to input this. Instead, their conceptual forms are initially hand-carved by the modelmaker from Modelab, a solid block of pink, high-density urethane resin. Shuttleworth describes this as a probing attempt to sculpt the form by ' . . . attacking the material with cutting and sanding machines'. The prototype will then function as a prelude to a series of consultations between modelmaker and designer from which successive and evolving versions ultimately fine-tune the form that, hitherto, existed only in the imagination of the architects.

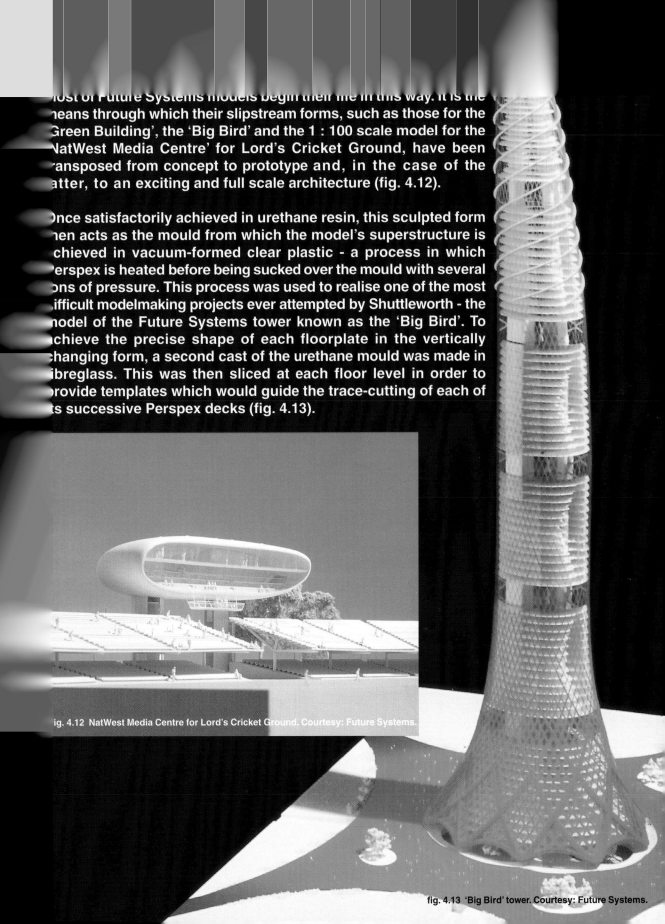

Most of Future Systems models begin their life in this way. It is the means through which their slipstream forms, such as those for the 'Green Building', the 'Big Bird' and the 1 : 100 scale model for the NatWest Media Centre' for Lord's Cricket Ground, have been transposed from concept to prototype and, in the case of the latter, to an exciting and full scale architecture (fig. 4.12).

Once satisfactorily achieved in urethane resin, this sculpted form then acts as the mould from which the model's superstructure is achieved in vacuum-formed clear plastic - a process in which Perspex is heated before being sucked over the mould with several tons of pressure. This process was used to realise one of the most difficult modelmaking projects ever attempted by Shuttleworth - the model of the Future Systems tower known as the 'Big Bird'. To achieve the precise shape of each floorplate in the vertically changing form, a second cast of the urethane mould was made in fibreglass. This was then sliced at each floor level in order to provide templates which would guide the trace-cutting of each of its successive Perspex decks (fig. 4.13).

fig. 4.12 NatWest Media Centre for Lord's Cricket Ground. Courtesy: Future Systems.

fig. 4.13 'Big Bird' tower. Courtesy: Future Systems.

Vacuum-forming is used by Unit Twenty Two for both large and small model components; forms exceeding the capacity of their in-house thermoform machine being produced at Pinewood Film Studios. By contrast, the intricacy of their model of 'The Ark' - Future Systems' spectacular building for the Earth Centre campus in Doncaster - involved each of the tiny, calibrated 'eye' segments being individually vacuum-formed in clear plastic. These were then trimmed with a scalpel and, before colour-spraying, painstakingly mounted and glued into position on the curvature of the two vacuum-formed lenses (fig. 4.14).

Although Shuttleworth accepts the direct correlation between the vacuum-forming process and the biomorphic nature of his clients' designs, many of his models can result from a mixed palette of materials including Perspex, urethane, MDF, resin, brass, etc: combinations of materials demanding an equally complex range of gluing mediums including dichloromethane, superglues and epoxy resins. However, once finished with filler paste, sanded, and then completely sprayed white using matte cellulose paint, the disparate assembly is homogonised into a single entity.

fig. 4.14 Vacuum Formed 'lenses'. The Ark. Courtesy: Future Systems.

More recently, colour has emerged as an important issue, and Shuttleworth feels that he made some contribution to this move away from the pristine. Hitherto, small areas of Future Systems' models could be coloured but this selectivity has now given way to experiments using fluorescent pinks and yellows over the complete model envelope. Shuttleworth claims that this shift emanates from Kaplicky's deep fascination with the process of modelmaking and the rapport that has developed between them. However, the introduction of colour, together with the various surface effects required in the model, can often demand an extremely complex masking procedure that is more akin to the airbrush painting technique (fig. 4.15).

There also exists a similarity of size in these models but their overall baseboard sizes are similar. This similarity, according to Shuttleworth, is governed more by physical size and the attendant ability to pass through doors and into taxi's when being transported to the many meetings.

fig. 4.15 The Ark, Earth Centre, Doncaster. Courtesy: Future Systems.

fig. 4.16a Hôtel du Département Marseilles, Alsop & Störmer.
© Andrew Putler.

Richard Armiger: The Network Modelmakers

After studying sculpture in his native Baltimore, Richard Armiger worked for a spell as a photographer in the Boston-based Cambridge Seven Associates. Here, he became intrigued by the architects' approach to design and, especially, their use of crude but honest models to develop three-dimensional ideas. Later, he left for England to study modelmaking at the Kent Institute of Art & Design under George Rome Innes. Then followed a period making in-house models for Casson Condor Architects, Ove Arup and Partners and BBC Special Effects before setting up his modelmaking firm The Network in 1983.

Armiger is intensely proud of his art background and sees architectural modelmaking as a perfect marriage between sculpture and building. He considers the model as first and foremost a piece of sculpture, i.e., as being inspirational, representative and true to material. Furthermore, all those issues that apply to sculpture - issues such as innovation, materiality and symbolism - also apply to modelmaking. At a time when the industry has become so fiercely competitive and many firms standardise their modelmaking approach, he strives to achieve models that are unique to each architect and inspirational to each project. For instance, many firms used standard colours for their models, but Armiger always mixes colours for each project and he is often given a free hand so to do. Indeed, according to Armiger: 'Architects are amazingly scared of colour' which he puts down to the widespread fashion for white and silver models. As a consequence, his artistic, 'one-off' approach - often made keener by the leanness of budgets and tightness of deadlines - does not confine him to one or two clients. Rather, his client portfolio is composed of an impressive array of the more adventurous architects including those headed by David Chipperfield, John McAslan and Nicholas Grimshaw, etc., and each of them will request, even demand, that their project be given a singular individuality.

Armiger describes the architectural model as having a life beyond the obvious: models eliciting decisions from clients, functioning as refential talismen in the ensuing design process and embodying a publicity value. For instance, among his most internationally published work are two very different models. One is that for Will Alsop's competition-winning 'Big Blue' for Marseilles - which achieved exposure in *Newsweek*. The other is his beautifully restrained wooden model for David Chipperfield's proportionally sensitive John Kao House in Boston (figs. 4.16a & 4.16b).

fig. 4.16b John Kao House. © Andrew Putler.

Exhibition work has always been important to Armiger, and each year since 1983 his models have been selected for display at the Royal Academy of Arts Summer Exhibition. Also, exhibitions of the work of modern masters, such as Le Corbusier, Adolf Loos and Frank Lloyd Wright have benefited from the thoroughness of his research. For example, Armiger describes the case of Le Corbusier's Villa Stein: 'The present building is nothing like the original design. Back in the fifties it was badly converted into four self-contained apartments. Although the Fondation Le Corbusier supplied us with microfiche copies of the original drawings, these contradicted the Yerbury photographs taken in 1927 proving that even the greatest architects will change things for the better at the last possible moment! We first built the crudest of card models to test the scale and fixed points and, after piecing together information from six different sources, together with the Hayward Gallery's approval, we then felt confident enough to proceed with the final exhibition model (fig. 4.17).

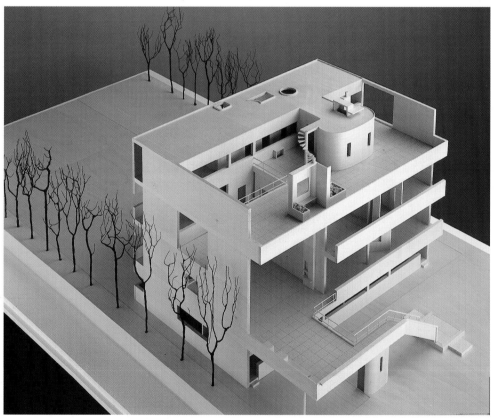

fig. 4.17 Villa Stein, Le Corbusier. © Andrew Putler.

However, it is Armiger's impressively successful track record in prestigious competitions that has established his reputation in the architectural fraternity. He recognises that a competition prototype is a very different 'animal' from the presentation model, describing it as a 'conceptual abstraction' usually built within a restricted budget between four to six days. In the case of competitions, he says, 'I first try to remind the architect-client that the model should do a whole lot more than merely verify the drawings. It should exist as the one element in a presentation to attract the most serious scrutiny, especially from laypeople. The main difficulty is to persuade the client to prioritise the model. The modelmaking programme is often squeezed. This will compromise the entry; not an ideal situation when the purpose is to win'. However, Armiger relishes the challenge, because ' . . . you can do a lot with a little and get lost with a lot. In competitions we tend to be lean and mean, and you don't get bogged down with detail'. The Network have a maxim: 'You can't polish a turd'. Armiger suggests that it becomes difficult when people try to enlist their expertise in order to pull the wool over people's eyes.

From among his many and shared successes is the model for Future Systems' sensual entry to the Bibliothèque de France competition, which achieved unofficial second place. There is also the conceptual model for John McAslan + Partner's winning competition entry for the Yapi Kredi Bankasi headquarters in Istanbul, Turkey. Armiger's interpretation of the latter resulted from sketches and conversations with the architects from which emerged his notional question: 'So, . . . it's just a big Noguchi lamp?' Consequently, after three intensive days in construction, Armiger's resulting model intuitively stayed with the notion of light transmission and, working from inside out, became a layered maquette using four different materials of varying translucency: tinted and clear acrylic, silver dry transfers, micron thin cedar wood and tracing paper (fig. 4.18).

fig. 4.18 Yapi Kredi Bankasi headquarters, John McAslan + Partners. © Andrew Putler.

Another first prizewinning entry is Armiger's 1997 competition model for David Chipperfield's redevelopment of Berlin's Neues Museum (fig. 4. 19). He is intensely proud of this model because it celebrates his admiration for and long-term relationship with Chipperfield. Indeed, their respective firms were each founded in the same year. Chipperfield's rigorous Modernist forms provide Armiger with a modelmaking challenge. 'The way David juxtaposes materials and carves out space is exceptional', he says, 'But when drawn flat in two dimensions it is dullness defined'. To make his minimalism sing, Armiger uses materials provocatively but sensitively. Paradoxically, Armiger's preference for impregnated rather than applied colour led him to construct the Neues Museum model in timber as was Chipperfield's preference. However, to satisfy the competition rules that stipulated a white model, he saturated it with water-based Artist's Colour. Options were also explored for representing the large areas of glazing; the solution being a triple lamination of clear, etched and tinted acrylic. Finally, tiny abstracted Greek artifacts were positioned within the model which, when lit from lights mounted below, appeared as ghost-like silhouettes.

fig. 4.19 Neues Museum, Berlin. David Chipperfield Architects. © Putler/Armiger.

More recently, Rick Mather's delicate and prize-winning proposals for the South Bank Revisited competition also included an uplit schematic model by Armiger. Built against the clock in 'Cibatool' and acrylic laid over a light box, the model was to succeed against powerful entries from architects such as Michael Hopkins and Rem Koolhaas, Mather's success illustrates another aspect of Armiger's work, i.e., his careful research into the nature of the presentation setting and his recognition of that psychological moment when first impressions are formed. He never underestimates the importance of that highly-charged moment when a design is seen in a three-dimensional form for the first time. There is also a presentation issue that recognises the precise role of each component of a competition submission. For example, models, drawing types, photographs, etc., should always complement rather than duplicate each other. Equally important is the size and shape of the presentation room together with the number of judges and any planned seating arrangement. 'In the case of the South Bank competition, with 22 judges to address, there was little point in turning up with a power-book-sized model. If they can't see the presentation material, you have blown it in an instant!'

The scale used by Armiger for this competition was an odd one, i.e., 1 : 850. It was chosen to provide the best balance of opposites: large enough to exert maximum impact and physical presence but, apart from suggesting rather than prescribing detail, small enough to allow inclusion of the key landmarks on the enormous site.

Armiger assumes the role of candid and unofficial modelmaker's spokesman. He insists that modelmakers make an enormous contribution to the design process and to the realisation of a building project - from conception, through development and refinement to client persuasion. The realisation of architecture rarely happens without their contribution and the fact that they are seldom recognised needs to be addressed. He concludes: 'Our industry has a tremendous record. Every significant building was first tested in three dimensions with a modelmaker as one of the team. A great modelmaker must be a good team player but, when the credits roll, it is very disheartening when acknowledgement of our contribution is omitted'.

However, modelmaker's are keenly aware that, once photographed, the model becomes transposed from the scaled miniaturism of its Lilliputian world and into one that sees it assuming human-scale proportions within the illusion of the two-dimensional plane. Furthermore, this transposition removes the model from the hands of its maker for a scrutiny through the lens of the model photographer - and its subjection to yet another range of skills found along its life as a communication tool.

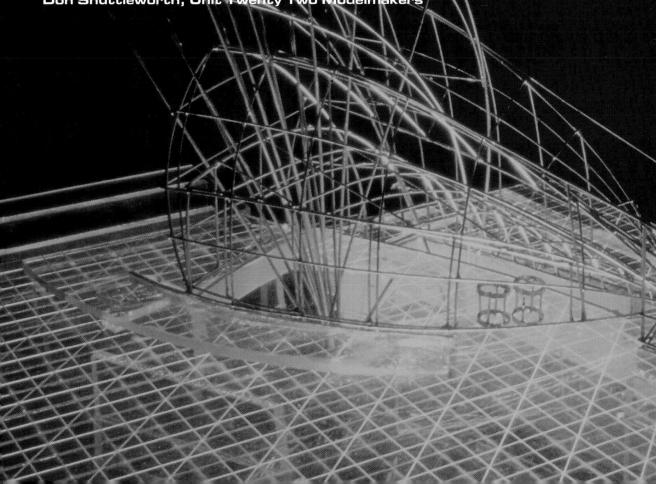

5

Shooting for Reality

'Photographs (of models) are very important. Most people do not see the model. What they see is a photograph and it is important that the model is built in a manner that it can be photographed, i.e., it must be able to adapt itself to achieving various shots.'

Don Shuttleworth, Unit Twenty Two Modelmakers

Our visual experience of space and form relies upon a hierarchy of optical functions that are triggered by visual contact with the real world. Known as depth cues, these are the perceptual signals, such as 'perspective', 'overlap' and 'size differential', etc. Although we utilise these signals to create illusions of space in pictorial representation, two important and primary visual cues are always missing. The first is binocular vision which refers to the fact that each of our eyes receives a slightly different image from the object in view, and the ability of our two eyes to focus on only one point at a time - whether it be near or far away. Our eyes also give overlapping fields of view and stereoscopic depth vision; motions of the head and eyes giving rise to the secondary primary depth cue - motion parallax. Motion parallax results from movement at right-angles to a line of vision that alters the relative positions of two unequally distant objects, such as the relative movement of nearer trees and distant hills seen from a speeding train.

Therefore, if we compare the representational prowess of a two dimensional image with a physical model we can see that, albeit existing at a diminished scale, the latter, in embodying all of the primary and secondary visual depth cues, can be seen to be closer to perceived reality. Indeed, other sensory receptors are involved, such as the sense of touch and smell. It is our ability to move around, to feel or to handle the model that many designers see as the key advantage when marketing a proposed design to a client. However, despite its multi-sensory presence, the physical model will invariably revert to the pictorialism of the two-dimensional image. This is done for several reasons, such as the need to reach a wider audience. It is an important transformation into a medium that, surprisingly, can be more critical than the physical construction itself. This is because, essentially, we are 'visual animals'; conditioned by the media screen and page into accepting two-dimensional events as true versions of reality - a well-considered and well-taken photograph enhancing the model and converting it into a more 'lifelike' and perceptually 'realistic' experience. Furthermore, even more so than its physical counterpart which provides no more than a view of its formal entirety, a sequence of well-conceived photographs can provide a clearer understanding of the spirit of the design. This medium transfer is endorsed by Andrew Ingham of Andrew Ingham & Associates who suggest that one does have to encourage people to view models in a particular way: 'The main drawback of models is that you end up looking at roofs all the time, which in reality is the last thing you are going to see'.

Through a use of photography the modelmaker becomes movie director, i.e., controlling the viewing experience through orchestrating lighting conditions, angle and frame and cropping of view, etc., so that only the shots that convey the essence of the design are recorded and published. Furthermore, the act of photographing a small object and blowing-up the resultant image into a large format adds a new perceptual dimension. Not only does this act transfer the model to a medium associated with reportage and actuality, it consciously eliminates problems of scale and allows us to escape our fascination with miniaturism; a fascination that heightens the discrepancy between human and model scales that keeps us outside of the spatial world of the model. For instance, if we now compare the perception of the scale model with that of the real world, we discover that it is the very primary depth cues that can exert an adverse effect on our understanding of its intentions. Due to the visual voracity of the binocular parallax depth cue (disparity resulting from the fact that each eye receives a slightly different image from a perceived object in focus) we can experience too much vision. For example, if we look at a pencil held near our face, due to is size in relation to the distance between our eyes, it is possible to see slightly more than half-way around its stem: now imagine that the pencil represents a building component, say a column in model form. So we can understand that when viewing a complete model of a building, our field of vision can absorb a far greater amount of spatial information than when viewing an actual building. The viewing of models with our naked eyes, therefore, can induce binocular distortion - the interocular distance between our eyes emphasising the difference in scale.

The distance interposed by rich displays of spatial intracacy is known as the 'Gulliver Gap', or 'toytown syndrome', i.e., an awareness of our own physical size and bulk in relation to that of a scale model. Artists are fully aware of the fact that the significance of an idea in cartoon or maquette form may be lost or reduced when enlarged to full-size; as the scale of a painting, a sculpture, and a building is increased, so too the amount of information within the field of vision reduces proportionally - often relegating a seemingly exciting idea to the mundane. As a means of compensation, many architects make models large enough to accept the head and so simulate interior eye-level views. Another technique for bridging the scale barrier is the endoscope, or modelscope. This transports the mind's eye directly into a model space. Modelscopes are miniature periscopes which, when inserted into models, can function as design tools by providing visual access to selective and realistic eye-level images. Perceived movement through model-space can also be simulated by the simple operation of panning and tracking. These views can be photographed by attaching a camera to the modelscope but the resulting circular photographs tend to be of rather poor quality with distortion occurring around the edge.

The attachment of a miniature video camera to the modelscope allows a filmed real-time movement through and around the model. Using overhead motorised gantries, model-video movies became a popular medium in the eighties when both private and university-based simulation centres had been established across Europe and America. But, overtaken by a digital technology by the early nineties many of these, such as the Bouwcentrum in Rotterdam and the Environmental Simulation Laboratory at Berkeley, California, have been disbanded. Others - as in the world of space and aeronautic flight simulation - have transferred from camera-on-model displays to computer-generated animation. But, recent developments in fibre optics connects a video camera probe with a thermal printer. For instance, the Elmo EM102 that will efficiently and cheaply print-out one-size prints in black-and-white or colour of the image seen and selected on the monitor as a monochrome print.

However, shooting directly images of a model from a monitor screen involves its own discipline. Motion pictures, such as video, projected movie film or television pictures rely upon the ability of the human eye to separate rapidly sequentially presented still images - a television image, for example, being completely reformed 30 times per second. This means that to photograph a televised picture at shutter speeds slower than 1/30 or 1/25 second will not record the complete image. Consequently, when shooting from a television screen one should always use a shutter speed of 1/8 or 1/5 second. Moreover, this type of photography always needs to be shot using a tripod, as shutter speeds lower than 1/60 second, if hand-held, will result in camera 'shake'and an attendant loss of focus in the resultant print.

Depending upon the scale and accessibility of the model, good photographic results can be achieved using an SLR (Single Lens Reflex) camera (fig. 5.1). When working with the camera it is worth contemplating two shooting sessions: the first exhaustively explores the possibilities of image achievement; the second session using the first to inform a more determined sequence of photographs. Intended qualities of light and space should be investigated during the first shoot by orchestrating spotlights or floodlights to control the intensity, focus and direction of illumination and, indeed, to maximise the theatre of the photographic event.

fig. 5.1 'Alice in Wonderland' Virtual Reality Centre, Diploma student 1:200 scale design model.
Courtesy: Rick Hall and Alex Masheder.

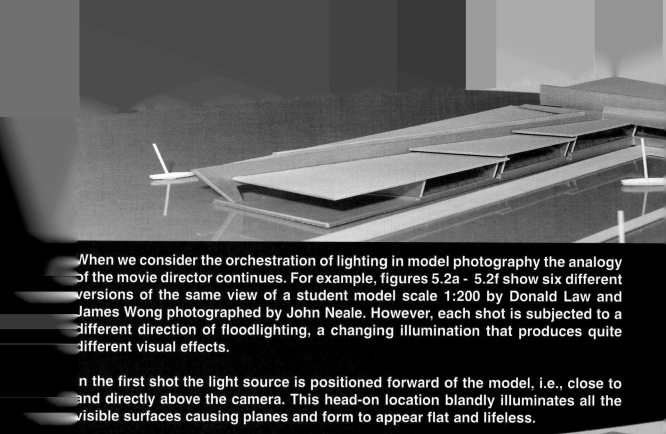

When we consider the orchestration of lighting in model photography the analogy of the movie director continues. For example, figures 5.2a - 5.2f show six different versions of the same view of a student model scale 1:200 by Donald Law and James Wong photographed by John Neale. However, each shot is subjected to a different direction of floodlighting, a changing illumination that produces quite different visual effects.

In the first shot the light source is positioned forward of the model, i.e., close to and directly above the camera. This head-on location blandly illuminates all the visible surfaces causing planes and form to appear flat and lifeless.

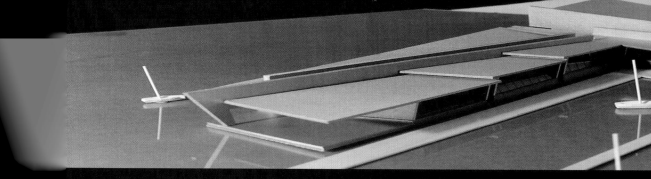

In the second shot the light source is positioned to the left of the model, a position that, while maintaining detail, induces a much greater visual contrast. On the one hand, this photograph creates a strong sense of three dimensions while, on the other hand, it exploits the glowing qualities of light reflected back into shadowed planes. The third shot results from the light source being moved slightly behind the model while still occupying a position to its left. While losing some sense of detail, the resultant image is high in tonal contrast and visual drama.

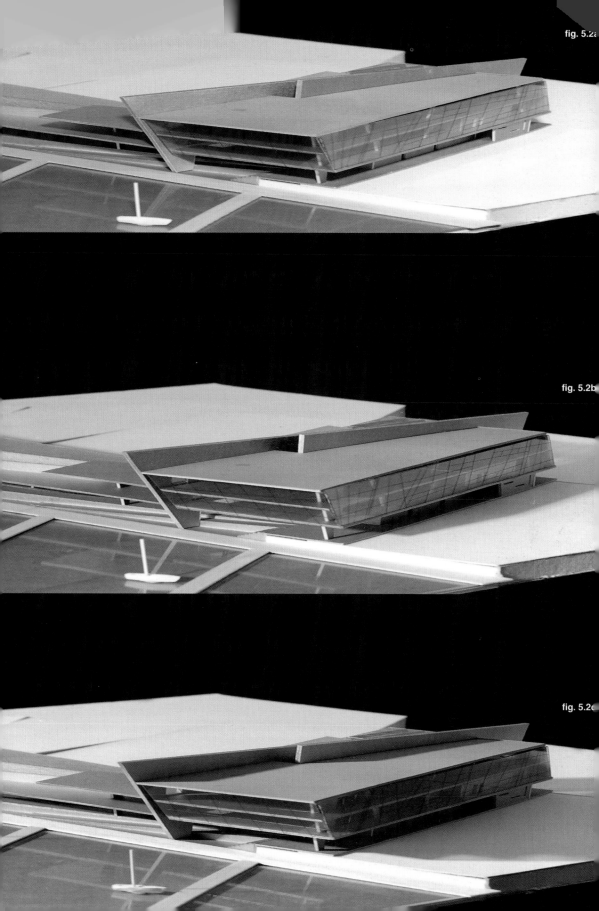

fig. 5.2a

fig. 5.2b

fig. 5.2c

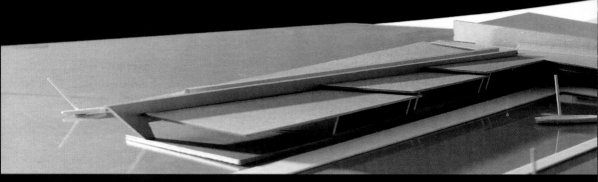

The light source is again moved for the fourth shot, being lowered immediately behind the model. This time the bulk of architectural mass is emphasised at the expense of any detailed disclosure. Also, rather than receiving direct light, those planes that remain illuminated rely more on light that is reflected back into the model. In the fifth shot the light source is elevated to a point directly facing the camera lens and causes a diffused image that is softened by flared light which is bounced back into the model from the rear wall. Finally, in the sixth shot, the light source is lowered and hidden behind the model until a complete silhouette is achieved.

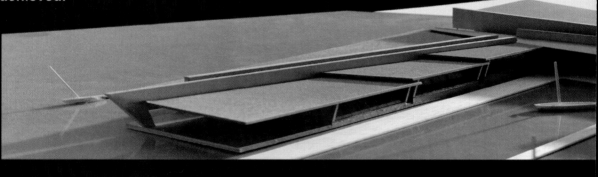

The intention of this demonstration is not to promote any particular attitude when photographing models. Rather, it is intended to illustrate some of the basic and achievable effects. Also, it is always wise to experiment with different qualities and directions of light so that the model can be optimised during a photographic session. This is because it is the unplanned and accidental shot that can often capture the unexpected power of an architectural model.

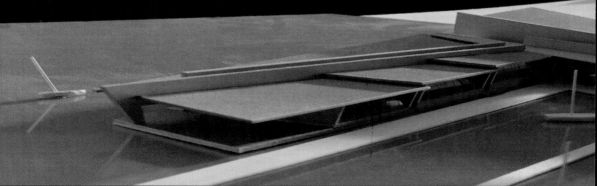

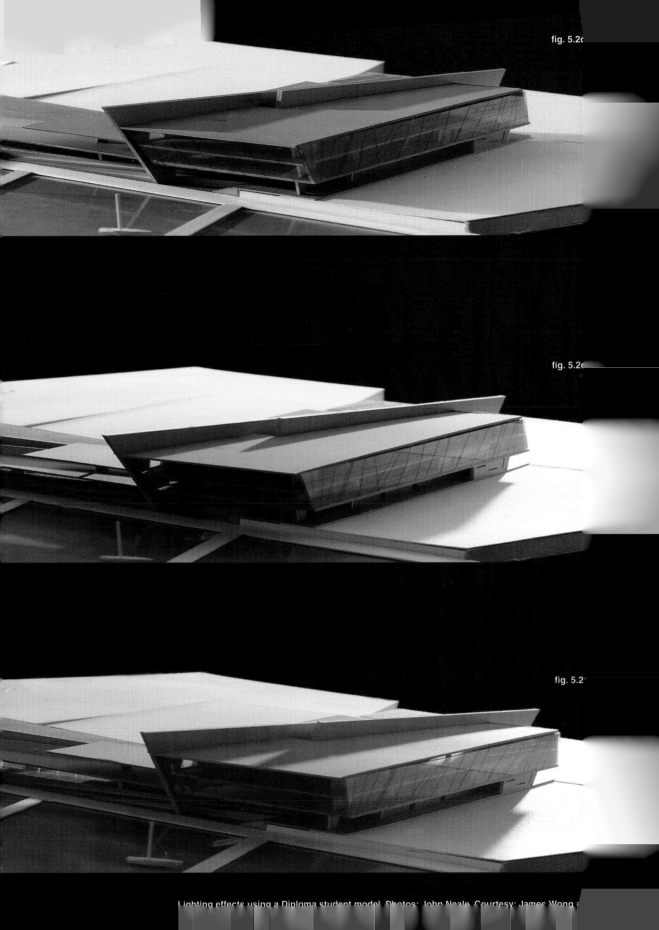

fig. 5.2d

fig. 5.2c

fig. 5.2

Lighting effects using a Diploma student model. Photos: John Neale. Courtesy: James Wong

A popular presentation image is a computer photomontage that superimposes a photograph of the model with that of a site (see fig. 3.8, page 56). This quest for contexuality sees shots taken of the site and of the model from vantage points that allow their fusion to take place. Many designers will also shoot the model outdoors against the sky or, alternatively, studio-photograph the model against a simulated sky backdrop (fig. 5.3).

fig. 5.3 The Network's scale 1 : 200 model of the Eden Project against
a sky backdrop. Courtesy: Nicholas Grimshaw & Partners.

Often, the illusion of reality imparted in photographs can be very impressive especially when they are processed as grainy, atmospheric prints. Such an effect is achieved in the New York and Paris based practice of Bernard Tschumi. Described by Tschumi as 'photograms' these are achieved by means of photographic prints taken from a large-scale in-house model which are then subjected to several reprographic transformations. For instance, the prints are first Xeroxed as black and white photocopies before being professionally rephotographed to a large scale using a process camera and printed on textured photographic paper at formats of up to 3 x 4'. Finally, in order to emphasise the main features of the design concept, the prints are touched-up using an airbrush.

fig. 5.4a

The resultant printed grain shows the model apparently bathed in the light of aerial perspective - a visual depth cue created when sunlight is scattered on dust particles in the atmosphere to cause a kind of 'digital' haze. Each step in the transformation reduces detail and softens hard edges in the original to imbue a convincing sense of scale (figs. 5.4a & 5.4b). The effect is heightened by incidental intrusions of light in the original photograph and accidental interferences in the transmutation process. These appear to enhance the desired impression, i.e., a scalar distancing of the model in space and the distancing of any evidence of the creator in the ultimate image. Indeed, the grainy print subtly shifts the standpoint of the viewer because in comparison to viewing the abstraction of an architectural drawing, he or she is taking part in an entirely plausible architectural event.

fig. 5.4b

Bibliothèque National de France photograms. Courtesy: Bernard Tschumi Architects.

Albeit in the context of high-resolution computer graphics, this trend towards the softer photographic image is echoed in the digitised images of Alan Davidson of Hayes Davidson. Frequently created while designs are still fluid, Hayes Davidson's superimposed photographic and electronic images can be merged into a perspective drawing or a site photograph as seamless, composite images. The work is used to test urban fit and proposed lighting conditions, etc. His renderings appear in newspaper articles and journals throughout the world and play their role in the wider public architectural debate (fig. 5.5).

Davidson observes that many people believe that photorealism means 'looking as it does in real life'; but it doesn't. A picture can, he says, be photorealistic yet appear unlike what we actually see. Davidson uses the term 'photoaccuracy' to describe the perception of what an image may look like in real life. In his creative work this involves a certain amount of diffusion and blurring and investing its content with what he calls a 'painterly feel'.

On the other hand, modelmaker David Gomm finds the computer-rendered image to be too soft and lacking in optical drama. He has made this critical assessment by directly comparing computer images with photographs of a physical model of the same building design sharing precisely the same viewpoint and vanishing points. Having seen several comparative images that have passed through his workshop, he concludes that computer renderings have to work extremely hard in order to compete with photographs of the model. This is because they do not appear to embody the degree of sharpness of detail and contrast in tone that our vision demands in order to instil visual credibility. It is this aspect that he feels vital when, in client presentations, the images of a virtual design should survive a searching scrutiny under extreme enlargement.

However, according to Thomas Fisher, to communicate a design in a recognisable manner, models can communicate on more than one level. But this does not mean that they must be entirely realistic. He writes: 'An object can be shown with all its flaws, or be idealised as if in a dream, or distorted according to our perception of it, or reduced to its essential formal or symbolic qualities. Each of these approaches carries a very different meaning, yet each still adheres in varying ways to the recognisable depiction of the object'.

fig. 5.5 Broad Street. Alan Davidson brings a painterly quality to his computer montages. © Hayes Davidson.

Andrew Putler

Emerging from a background of photographing rock-and-roll groups and jazz musicians in the late sixties, Andrew Putler is the doyen of architectural photographers. During the eighties he covered just about everything except fashion and social photography, but it was during this period - while shooting models of petrol stations and banks for Wolff Olins - that he first met Richard Armiger. It was Armiger who persuaded him to focus more on architectural model photography and a fruitful collaboration ensued. For example, Putler's photographs of Armiger's celebrated model of Alsop & Störmer's 'Grande Bleu' in Marseilles, and his shots of Dixon Jones' winning entry to the Venice Gateway competition - together with other entries including those from the practices of Harper Mackay and Eva Jiricna - attracted extensive publicity. Architects now turn to Putler for an image of their model that will function as an icon of their project - his widespread reputation emanating from continued success in transforming the architectural maquette from a three-dimensional object into a highly persuasive and visually compelling event (fig. 5.6).

fig. 5.6 Daniel Libeskind's Spiral, Victoria & Albert Museum. Model by Millennium Models. © Andrew Putler.

Working from his dedicated, home-based studio, Putler begins with the architect's brief that usually includes the model's orientation and prescribed range of basic views. Artistic freedom will result from his rapport with the architect and how well the brief is communicated. For instance, when Terry Farrell & Partners' model of 'The Deep' arrived, Putler was briefed to make very low, broadside shots in order to focus on the drama of the its orientation and reflected structure. Beyond this requirement he was invited to follow his own instincts.

A typical shoot commences with the choice of background colour and how well this hue works with the general palette of the model. Lighting the models begins with the all-important 'key light' - its positioning in terms of height and direction being critical to the drama of the eventual photograph. The key light is then counterbalanced using either a reflector or an auxillary soft light to provide 'fill-in' illumination. Thereafter, the horizon has to be illuminated in order to differentiate the model from the background. If the model incorporates its own integral lighting, this will have to be colour-corrected with gels or substituted with flash or tungsten lighting. Putler finds the most exciting illumination to be that projected from low level, i.e., the quality and heightened colour and contrast of light occurring at dusk or dawn. For instance, in the case of 'The Deep' the most stunning image resulted from the jewel-like quality of simulated twilight beamed horizontally through the translucency of its tilted plates (fig. 5.7).

fig. 5.7 'The Deep.' Terry Farrell & Partners. © Andrew Putler.

121

Colour is a hallmark of Putler's photography and its orchestration via coloured gels plays an important part in their achievement. Indeed, as an antidote to the perpetual Technicolor blue skies found in professional model photography, his colour deployment is intensely theatrical with washed backdrops of evocative sunscapes using rich Indian reds and purples - the latter hue first used on Armiger's model of Le Corbusier's Ronchamp Chapel to create the shock of a different image (fig. 5.8). However, he will invariably shoot a whole range of shots which experiment with colour and light from the dramatically moody and atmospheric to the more conventionally sunlit or moonlit.

fig. 5.8 Le Corbusier's Ronchamp Chapel. Model by The Network. © Andrew Putler.

Putler works with a Sinar plate camera and a Nikon F3. When using the latter, shots are bracketed across a stop-and-a-half range. Modern film emulsions, especially Fuji, produce high-quality 35mm transparencies that can be enlarged to A3 prints. He will use three or four different lenses - sometimes enlisting a perspective shift (corrective) lens or, for getting in close to the model with views into its interior, a wide-angle lens. For the more prescriptive interior views (sometimes required for planning applications) he will use a fully-focusable modelscope with its 5mm prism. It is during these latter sessions, prodding and probing the model, when he describes himself as functioning a little like an ENT (Ear, Nose and Throat) specialist! Meanwhile, the telephoto lens, albeit interposing distance, imports its own kind of intimacy and is reserved for when the building form or an architectural detail needs to be separated, i.e., visually detached from its background. A favourite lens, however, is the 20mm wide-angle. This creates the illusion of being inside the space and although unwieldy and difficult to work with when getting in close to models below a scale of 1 : 50, he finds this lens holds the potential of suddenly bringing the model to life (figs. 5.9a & 5.9b).

fig. 5.9a Staircase. Eva Jiricna Architects. Model by The Network. © Andrew Putler.

fig. 5.9b Yapi Kredi Bankasi headquarters interior, Turkey.
John McAlsan + Partners. © Andrew Putler.

Whether functioning on an investigatory level in the design process, as a competition entry, to communicate a planning application, to attract investment or to market a finalised design proposal, models are essential tools. Putler sees the photographer's role as that of creating the best possible image in order to fulfil each purpose - the result of a shoot being processed as transparencies, prints or, using a digital camera, in electronic format. Design development models can often be crudely built and present a photographic challenge as, tending to draw the eye to their inaccuracies, they can provide unwanted centres of attention. Essentially, Putler is an intuitive photographer-approaching each subject, not as a model or a miniature building, but as an object, i.e., as a 'still life' to be photographed in order to accomplish the best 'look' and the most eye-catching image (fig. 5.10).

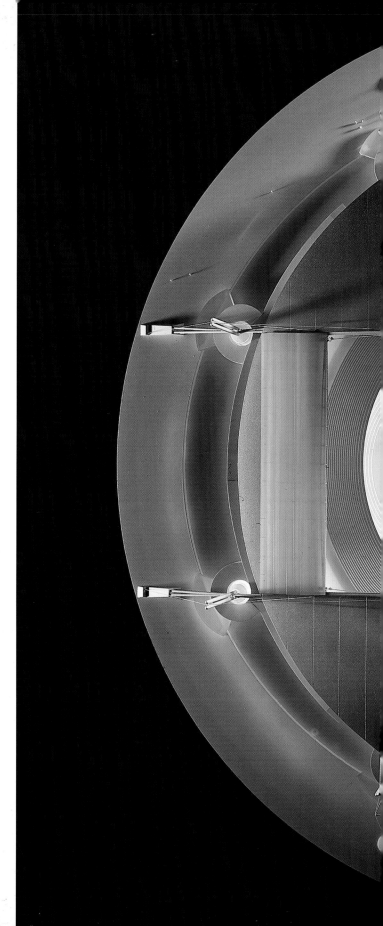

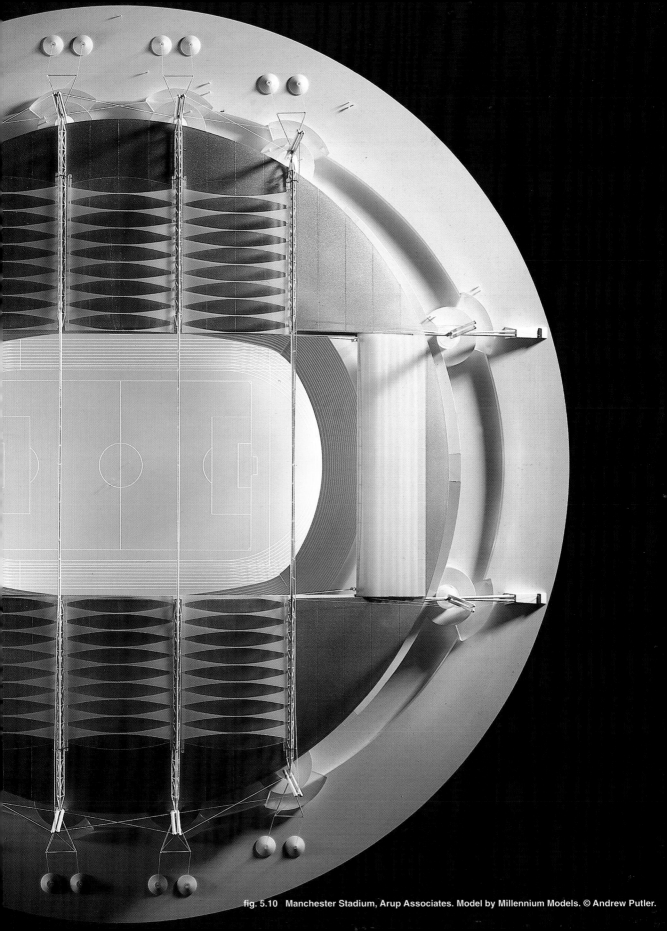

fig. 5.10 Manchester Stadium, Arup Associates. Model by Millennium Models. © Andrew Putler.

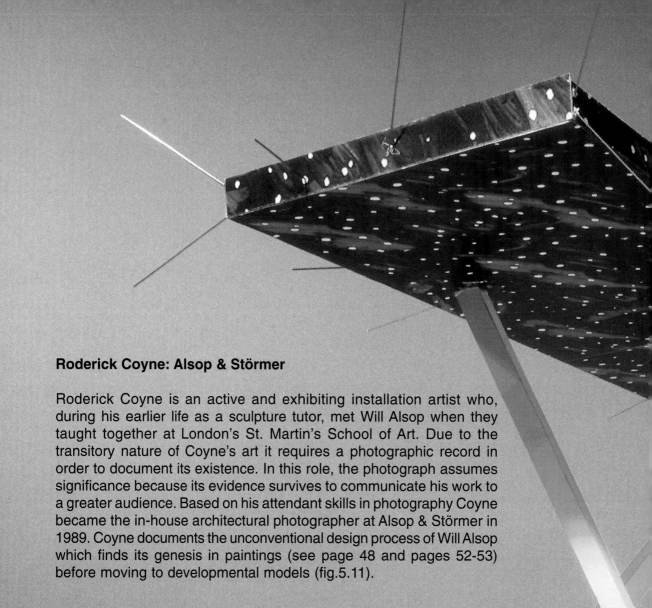

Roderick Coyne: Alsop & Störmer

Roderick Coyne is an active and exhibiting installation artist who, during his earlier life as a sculpture tutor, met Will Alsop when they taught together at London's St. Martin's School of Art. Due to the transitory nature of Coyne's art it requires a photographic record in order to document its existence. In this role, the photograph assumes significance because its evidence survives to communicate his work to a greater audience. Based on his attendant skills in photography Coyne became the in-house architectural photographer at Alsop & Störmer in 1989. Coyne documents the unconventional design process of Will Alsop which finds its genesis in paintings (see page 48 and pages 52-53) before moving to developmental models (fig.5.11).

fig. 5.11 Development model for c/Plex project, Alsop & Störmer. © Roderick Coyne.

fig. 5.12a

Development models for c/Plex project, Alsop & Störmer. © Roderick Coyne.

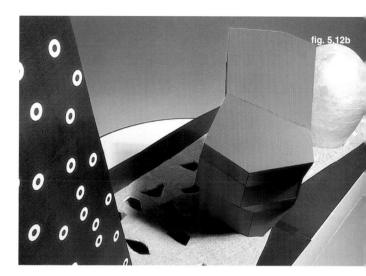
fig. 5.12b

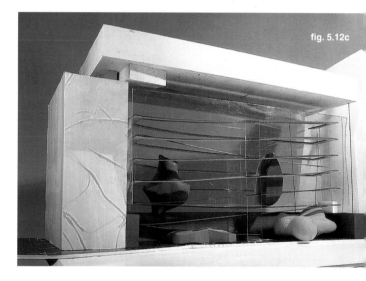
fig. 5.12c

He finds that the unresolved nature and expressiveness exhibited by, especially, the sketch models allows the camera licence to make its own contribution to the design debate (figs. 5.12a, 5.12b, 5.12c & 5.12d). For this reason he finds them the most exciting of subjects and is invariably on hand to shoot them.

fig. 5.12d

fig. 5.13a Development model for Swansea Literature Centre. © Roderick Coyne.

The result provides files of colour slides that function as a visual commentary on the models which, in successive design stages, become more and more refined; the procedure culminating in several presentation models which, themselves, can become increasingly fine-tuned as the debate continues (figs. 5.13a, 5.13b, 5.13c & 5.13d). Coyne's dossier of model images is, itself, a design tool that provides feedback to the ensuing design process. He believes that photographs play a

fig. 5.13b Development model for Hanover 2000. © Roderick Coyne.

fig. 5.13c Development model for Düsseldorf Hafen. © Roderick Coyne.

profound role in our culture - the picture providing a datum from which one can judge and review what has been achieved. Both the sculptor and the architect engage with three-dimensional form but it is the photographic version of the form that connects their work with the rest of our culture. In other words, we are conditioned to read events as framed by the viewfinder.

fig. 5.13d Development model for library block, Oosterdocks Eiland, Holland. © Roderick Coyne

fig. 5.14 'Barrow' (1997) 40 x 17' projection installation by Roderick Coyne. © Roderick Coyne.

Coyne describes his own art as concerned with framing. Indeed, as a prelude to an installation he will often make a scale model of the recipient gallery space - the gallery in which they are to be housed acting as a 'frame' for his work (fig. 5.14).

Similarly, buildings function as frames to the world outside. Furthermore, our experience of architecture is via the framed, published print - any comparison of two extraordinary buildings being undertaken only through the photographic medium. Coyne continues: 'We all trade in rectangular frames. My role here is to photographically snatch at the fleeting evidence of a developing design, i.e., to fix and frame the model in space'.

Model photography at Alsop & Störmer's is conducted in a makeshift studio using three light sources: a strong, primary, directional halogen lamp for the object-model; a secondary halogen lamp for washing the sky background and a low wattage tungsten modelling lamp to fill-in

some of the darker shadows. Shooting extensively and exclusively with his 35mm Nikon fitted with a shift lens, Coyne deliberately seeks out vantage points that will provide alternatives to the architectural emphasis and experience of the model. 'Very often aspects of the model are not apparent until one takes a photograph of it; based on the photographic view, designers can then see other possibilities'. By objectifying the nature of the model, it is the revelation of these future possibilities that Coyne sees as the great value of his photography in the process of design (fig. 5.15).

fig. 5.15 Development model, Alsop & Störmer. © Roderick Coyne.

Edward Woodman

Edward Woodman started his career in the early sixties working in the darkroom of a firm of photographers and commercial artists. By the middle of the decade he became a freelance photographer shooting for youth magazine features and interview portraits for *Campaign.* Later, by the end of the decade, he turned to photographing interiors and working as a freelance assistant to a specialist car photographer. Woodman describes this shift in subject-matter as coinciding with a gradual disillusionment with news values and generally moving away from photographing people to photographing objects together with a greater concern with form and its lighting. After a break from photography in the mid-seventies, Woodman returned as a still photographer for television news but the turning point came when in 1981 Sandy Nairne asked him to photograph sculptures for the ICA 'Objects & Sculpture' catalogue. It was during this time he met Zaha Hadid when he photographed her acrylic paintings as part of her prizewinning The Peak project. Later, Hadid invited him to photograph her models; since then he has almost exclusively been associated with her work.

Woodman's approach to photographing Hadid's models is not primarily to make them look like fake real buildings. His interest in them is as objects - but objects possessing a relationship to a full-scale three-dimensional reality. His experience in television and also of observing location movie-making led to his exclusive use of tungsten lighting and, especially, a small focusing spotlight as a key light, i.e., one 'believable' light source against which all other sources become subservient. This approach, Woodman claims, goes against the trend in studio photography of the last thirty years which uses flash and, particularly, 'soft boxes' (light attachments that diffuse the light source). In order to emphasise form and surface quality, employing a strongly directional light results in a combination of brightly lit areas and deep shadows within which details can, if required, be revealed by smaller 'fill' lights or reflectors. Also, as Hadid's models are mainly built of translucent materials, such as Perspex and cast resins, these demand an intense illumination in order to induce internal reflections that, in turn, define the edges of planes. 'I attempt to show their jewel-like appearance' says Woodman, . . .

fig. 5.16a

fig. 5.16b

Cardiff Bay Opera House, Zaha Hadid Architects. © Edward Woodman.

. . .'They appear as little fantasies (figs. 5.16a & 5.16b) consequently, representing these small objects as anything other than objects in their own right seems entirely inappropriate'. Flying in the face of conventional notions of reality, Woodman describes the influence on his work of the randomness and surrealism of the art of the late Joseph Cornell. Cornell created small events in white boxes, i.e., three-dimensional and themed assemblages of found objects, akin to the work of Kurt Schwitters. Cornell's containers function as metaphors of the whole world; inhabited by strange items - a treasury of curiosities that are compelling to explore. Similarly, Woodman generally photographs models as discrete objects defined against the contextual detachment of a black background (fig. 5.17). Because it provides a greater depth of field - together with an increased speed and mobility of working - almost all of his model photography uses 35mm film taken on a Nikon F3 with a variety of lenses. This allows him to work extremely close to the model. Furthermore, there is also the difficulty in predicting the exposure that will be most expressive on reversal (slide) film - the cost of covering the same possibilities on larger format cameras being ten times greater.

Usually the architect carries a very clear idea of the appearance and qualities of the design. Consequently, while planning his shots he remains open to their need in terms of the kind of ultimate building, the sort of light they envisage and whether or not there is a need to exaggerate its perspective. Whatever the brief, however, Woodman will rehearse his shots visually with one eye closed. This is because human vision is steroscopic and all-embracing while, of course, the camera's eye is monocular.

On those occasions when models incorporate interior lighting other than tungsten, the multiple exposure technique is used. In this, one exposure is made of the tungsten light that is played on to the model. The studio lighting is then turned off and the internal model lighting turned on and - using compensatory colour filters - the double exposure is made. A third light source, if it exists, will require a triple-exposure. A further technique sometimes used by Woodman is the projection of textures and other images directly on to the surface of models. In this event the model is mainly lit by the light of the projection, and any supplementary lighting has to avoid interfering with or bleaching-out the projected-images. Also, as projector optical systems emit a cool, greenish light, some compensatory colour filters have to be introduced. A beautiful example of this technique is Woodman's recording of Zaha Hadid's dance space for the Charleroi Danses in Belgium. Not only did Hadid design the set for this installation but she also designed the costumes. Moreover, the projected image that washes the model depicts a painting by the architect (fig. 5.18).

A major strand of Woodman's work is photographing contemporary art and some of the problems encountered when shooting sculpture and installation art, such as the work of Richard Wilson, Mona Hatoum, Bill Viola, and Cornelia Parker, etc., have informed his model photography. It is to the notion of the model as part of an installation event and as the subject and recipient of projection that we now turn.

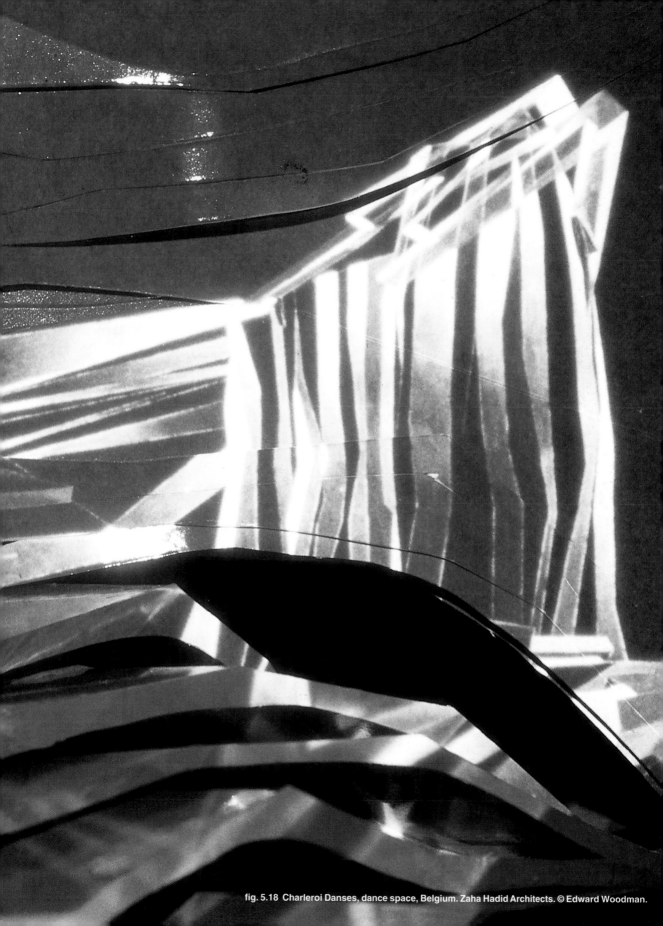

fig. 5.18 Charleroi Danses, dance space, Belgium. Zaha Hadid Architects. © Edward Woodman.

Even in the face of the power of the two-dimensional image, modelmakers uphold that it is the model's multi-sensory physical presence that functions as its salient selling point. They are convinced that the ability to walk around a model, to handle it, touch its surface and smell it is of paramount importance. However, the combination of film or slide projection and the model brings yet another experience - as well as the skills of the installation artist - to the process of communication. In order to understand this combination of mediums, one has only to experience the extraordinary power of projection exemplified in installations such as the Technoart exhibition in Berlin (figs. 5. 19a, 5.19b, 5.19c).

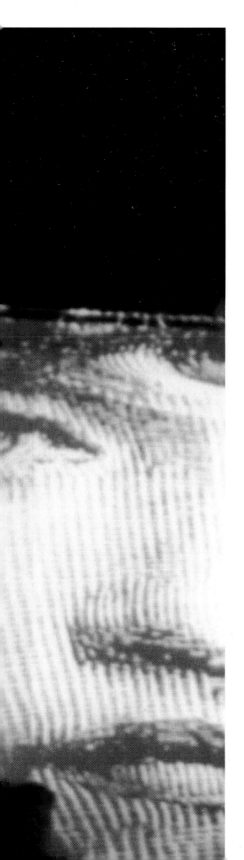

figs. 5.19a, 5.19b & 5.19c Technoart Exhibition, Berlin, 1995.
Projections by Skudi optics,
Abnorm and Exil(e).

143

By mixing the modelmaking craft with a projection technology, a whole new dimension in the experience of the architectural model is made possible. The act of projecting images onto maquettes or mock-ups not only reduces the isolation of the model, strengthens design concepts and provides a rich source for further photographs, but it also transforms the model into a test-bed for exploring new and exciting design avenues. Indeed, the superimposing of colour, text and patterns as layers of different information moves the experience of model into that of performance and event (fig. 5.20).

fig. 5.20 Imperial War Museum North. Daniel Libeskind. © Andrew Putler.

Such a combination of pictorial, literary and sculptural components is literally combined in some of the earlier models of Daniel Libeskind. Their entire surface is glue-laminated with words and images of found papers. For example, black text on white pages torn from Bibles and telephone directories denotes existing elements while the white-on-black of reversed prints of architectural drawings denotes the form and extent of the modelled intervention. The resulting coexistence of pictorial, sculptural and textual events involves a poetic dimension because, by including a collaged layer of signs and symbols in the wooden planes of the model, this fusion of language and form takes us to the very origins of Deconstructivism (figs. 5.21a & 5.21b).

fig. 5.21b Paper laminated model. Courtesy: Alsop & Störmer.
© Roderick Coyne.

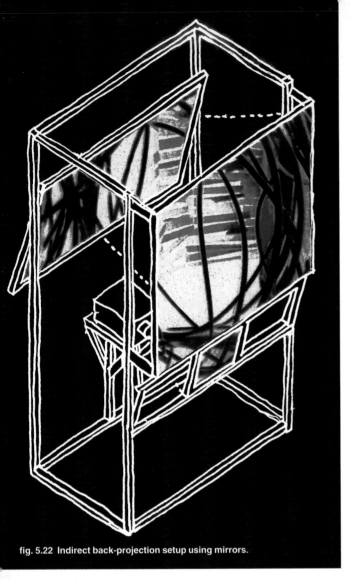

fig. 5.22 Indirect back-projection setup using mirrors.

Photographs of models can also be presented using a back projection setup. Indirect back projection can produce a reasonably large image over a comparatively short distance between projector and screen. This is achieved by using two mirrors: a smaller mirror placed near the project and a second the size of the required projection - nearer the screen (fig. 5.22). This compact projector-mirror-screen setup allows a clear and uninterrupted image that is back-projected from a small and concealed box behind the screen (fig. 5.23).

Back-projection screens can be made from a variety of different materials. For instance, a common 'screen' is made from heavy-duty tracing paper but one can also experiment with projection effects on calico, shrink-wrap plastic, sand-papered styrene and even Lutrasil (nappy liners) which induce a metallic appearance (fig. 5.24).

fig. 5.23 Back-projection.

fig. 5.24 Metallic effect of projected image using a Lutrasil screen .

Such installations include the multi-media 'working' walls and freestanding structures that have been designed and assembled by John Neale. Involving lighting techniques incorporating sensors and timers, back-projected movies and still images, models and part-models of varying scales and examples of actual building materials, etc., the distinction between model and design process becomes blurred (fig. 5.25). His installations represent an orchestration of techniques and technologies that are able to simultaneously convey a multiplicity of meaning. By mixing illusion with corporeality, his experiential structures hold the possibility of testing and communicating ideas at various scales, in various mediums and of bringing together different stages of design into one experience. Consequently, these installations become an integrated expression of the design process and, by taking us toward the reality-virtual reality interface, provide another means of 'shooting' for a sense of reality.

However, the final journey in the transformation of the model sees it manipulated and recreated in the virtual world of the computer. Therefore, it is to the encounter with the model in cyberspace that the concluding chapter is dedicated.

fig. 5.25 Mixed-media model installtion. John Neale.

Model in the Machine

'I like to think that computers will enhance physical model making, they will make it quicker, better and more accurate but, hopefully, not eliminate all the skills that are needed.' Chris Barber, Terry Farrell & Partners

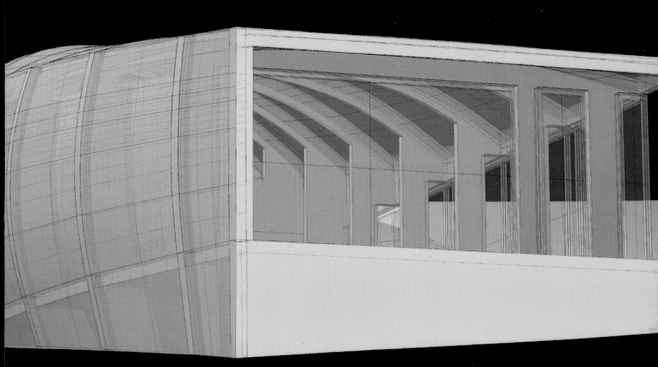

Computers are now common currency in most design practices. Twenty years ago it would have been hard to imagine just how commonplace a part of the architect's life they were destined to become. Today they are as familiar to designers as the stretched Whatman paper was to an earlier generation. This technological transfer can also be observed in the evolution of the multi coloured Lego building blocks with which, during infancy, so many architects first exercised their tectonic and modelmaking skills. A new generation of Lego, however, combines the familiar toy plastic brick with a built-in microcomputer to take the traditional system of building blocks into a high-tech range of 'intelligent' and interactive robot kits. A device transmits commands to the robots as infrared signals; the intelligent brick picks up the programs and uses signals from sensors to power the motors (fig. 6.1). Called 'Mindstorms' and developed in collaboration with MIT(Massachusetts Institute of Technology), this new generation of computer-driven 'modelmaking toy' not only sets new and challenging horizons for the child designer but, possibly, informs an emergent generation of designers who will be 'playing' with and 'inventing' the prototypes of a future and, possibly, responsive built environment.

fig. 6.1 Mindstorms Robotic Invention System. Courtesy: Lego.

Meanwhile, the most widely used CAD systems and software packages are those that are written specifically for the architectural profession and, thus, by serving to reinforce architectural preconceptions concerning form-making, tend to relegate the computer as a mere production tool. By borrowing from other disciplines, and using the machine for widely divergent objectives, some pioneering architects and designers driven by need to invent an architecture outside the precedent and beyond the norm are transcending this limitation.

These architects already embrace a new technology. For instance, rather than restrict the spatial technology offered by the computer to the role of visualiser and image-maker, they recognise that certain computer applications have radically redefined how we 'see' and conceptualise the making of space. Indeed, this re-establishment of the link between architectural design and a state-of-the-art technology provides a fresh opportunity for critical architectural exploration.

Primarily developed in the aerospace industry for the design of jet fighters, recent advances in electronics and CNC (Computer Numerically Controlled) technologies allow us to move directly from computer model/computer drawing to built form. This technology not only eliminates the distance between 'virtual' architectural hypotheses and the physical test of construction, but it also forces the architect to examine his or her role in a condition allowing greater potential input into the processing of building construction.

Since its general release, the technology has been adopted with dramatic results by the automative industry where it is now well-established. For instance, there are the rapid tooling centres, such as that at Styles Precision Components Limited on Teesside. Here, solid state stereolithographic machines, i.e., 3D machining packages using a laser to perfectly cut a computer-programmed solid from an epoxy resin medium, can rapidly tool block model prototypes directly from STL computer files sent down ISDN lines (Fig. 6.2). Once the prototype form is stereolithographically 'machined', the computer program that created the pattern can then be reapplied for a precise replication of its form in any required material, such as die cast aluminium or vacuum cast plastics, etc.

Also, in the US, the Chrysler Corporation have long since replaced the traditional and labour-intensive process of tediously hand-producing plywood-reinforced clay mock-ups for the research and development of new cars. Using this traditional technique neither aesthetics nor cost implication could be effectively assessed until these physical mock-ups were complete, and any resultant modification proved prohibitive.

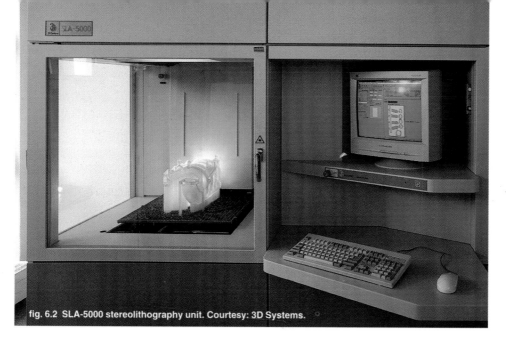

fig. 6.2 SLA-5000 stereolithography unit. Courtesy: 3D Systems.

Now, using software known as Catia, Chrysler designers sketch three-dimensional surfaces on the computer. Catia simultaneously translates the information into a geometric database that governs the milling machines that not only automatically produce the clay prototype but control the final manufacturing process. Consequently, after a decade with Catia, Chrysler have reduced their research and design cycle for new auto models from six years to just over two years!

A CNC technology is also adopted and in widespread use by professional modelmaking workshops but is mainly used for the mass production of small-scale and highly detailed components, such as staircases and window frames. However, an unusual and early example of this technology applied to modelmaking is found in the preparatory work for the exhibition *Leon Battista Alberti: the intellectual as architect* which toured Italy in 1994. Reconstructions at a scale of 1:20 of many of Alberti's surviving and unbuilt structures were built in Bergamo and Rome using computer models constructed by the Bath-and Edinburgh-based Alberti Group headed by Joseph Rykwert and Robert Tavernor. Based on historical data and new research, the computer models were produced using Olivetti 486 PCs running AutoCAD software. This was found to hold many advantages over previous reconstruction methods because, especially when representing Alberti's less well-documented projects and the more radically altered existing edifices, it allowed a comparative register of the differing versions. Furthermore, it also enabled an opportunity to accurately compare variant dimensions and proportional modules; the reconstructions, computer and physical models are illustrated and described in detail in Tavernor's book *On Alberti and the Art of Building*, 1998.

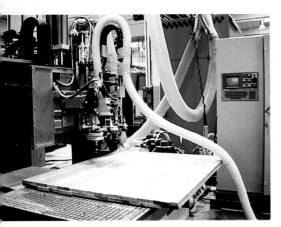

Rykwert's and Tavernor's digitised models were then converted by the Italian company CMS (Computer Mapping Services) using Olivetti pioneered CADCAM software designed originally to drive powerful cutting machines - the type usually employed for machining complex profiles out of stone. In order to check for any dimensional distortion that may have occurred in the data translation, the Alberti models were first prototyped in MDF (medium density fibreboard) (fig. 6.3). Finally, under the supervision of Professor Felice Ragazzo, the exhibition models were machined from pear wood (the material used by Renaissance modelmakers) to achieve an extremely high fidelity before being hand-finished by teams of traditional modelmakers (fig. 6.4a & 6.4b).

fig. 6.3 CNC modelling. Courtesy: Robert Tavernor.

fig. 6.4a

fig. 6.4b

figs. 6.4a & 6.4b CNC milled facade and detail. Courtesy: Robert Tavernor.

The wooden models were built more quickly and more cheaply than is usually the case, and were accompanied in the exhibition by rendered animations of the computerised models that had helped to build them.

However, degrees in the working relationship between the physical model and the digital model at the interface between the worlds of the actual and the virtual can be demonstrated in the respective design approaches of three quite different architectural practices: Branson Coates Architecture in London, Frank Gehry & Associates in Santa Monica, California and the work of William E. Massie in Bozeman, Montana.

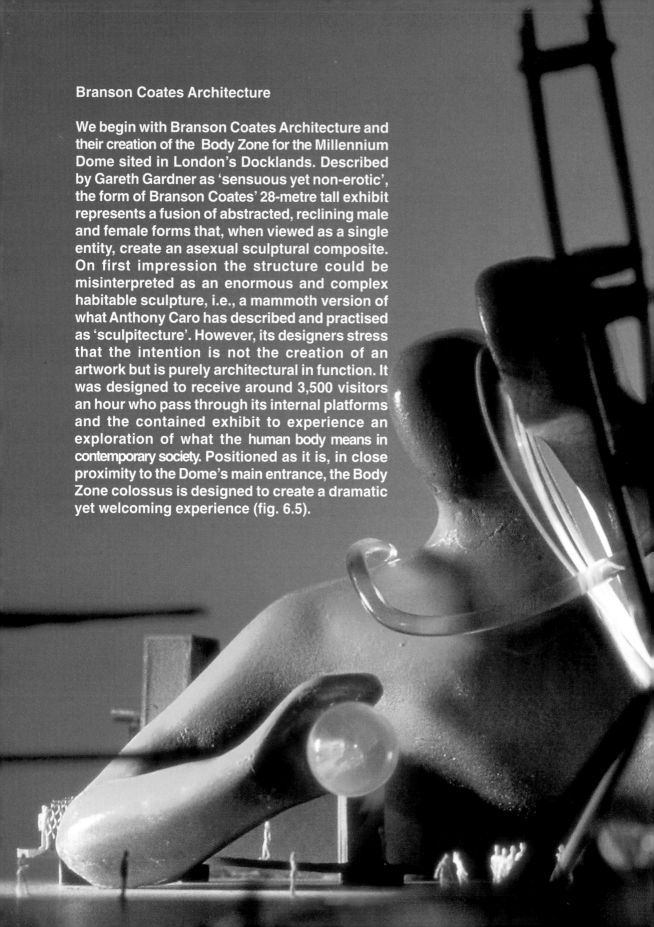

Branson Coates Architecture

We begin with Branson Coates Architecture and their creation of the Body Zone for the Millennium Dome sited in London's Docklands. Described by Gareth Gardner as 'sensuous yet non-erotic', the form of Branson Coates' 28-metre tall exhibit represents a fusion of abstracted, reclining male and female forms that, when viewed as a single entity, create an asexual sculptural composite. On first impression the structure could be misinterpreted as an enormous and complex habitable sculpture, i.e., a mammoth version of what Anthony Caro has described and practised as 'sculpitecture'. However, its designers stress that the intention is not the creation of an artwork but is purely architectural in function. It was designed to receive around 3,500 visitors an hour who pass through its internal platforms and the contained exhibit to experience an exploration of what the human body means in contemporary society. Positioned as it is, in close proximity to the Dome's main entrance, the Body Zone colossus is designed to create a dramatic yet welcoming experience (fig. 6.5).

fig. 6.5 Body Zone. Courtesy: Branson Coates Architecture. Photo: Guy Ryecart.

Working against the tight and intransigent deadline, the process began with Nigel Coates' initial concept of the reclining pose worked in two dimensions as a collage. This then became transferred into three dimensions with a sequence of nine or so exploratory clay maquettes - each modelled by Coates at small scale to refine the form of the last (fig. 6.6). However, these models were exclusively created to evolve the complex relationships of its formal mass. But, in order to work out how the figures would be constructed, and to produce drawings that would allow structural and cladding systems to be trialled, the physical model had to be digitised in the computer. In order to accomplish this Branson Coates used the same method as that employed at Terry Farrell & Partners for their Seoul Airport project (see pages 79-81). That is, the final model in the sequence was physically sectioned into 3mm slices - each slice then being scanned into the computer. The digitised sections were then reassembled by the machine to recreate the form as a CAD model.

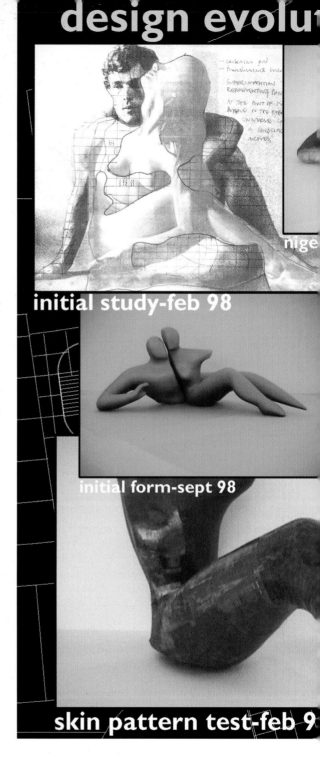

design evolu

initial study-feb 98

initial form-sept 98

skin pattern test-feb 9

model-feb 98   first plaster cast-april 98   structural hoop-june 98

ext model-oct 98   section model-jan 99

section model-jan 99

computer cut model-may 99   final skin pattern-may 99

fig. 6.6 Sequence of developmental models produced by Nigel Coates. Courtesy: Branson Coates Architecture.

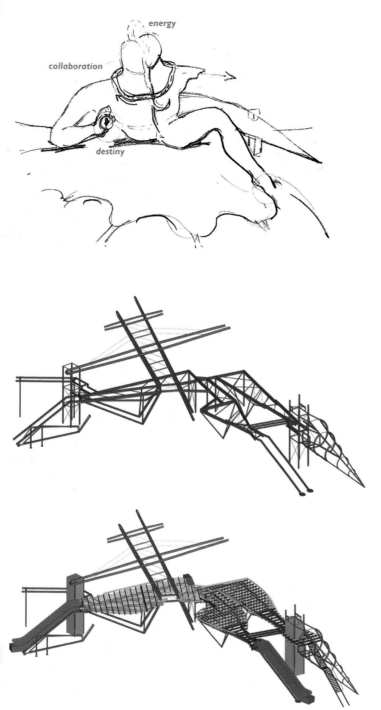

Working in close collaboration with the architects, the structural engineering consultancy, Buro Happold, ported the Branson Coates model into one generated on AutoCAD (release 14) that enabled the body's structure to be investigated. For example, after several different structural solutions had been explored, quickly established was the notion of a superstructure supporting a 'skeleton' formed by steel hoops bristling with delicate spacer bars whose tips both support and dictate the shape of a cladding system that acts rather like a 'skin' (fig. 6.7). Composed of a laminated outer layer of glass-reinforced concrete lightweight aerated concrete, the skin - like the underbelly of the Space Shuttle - is lined with tiles but, in this case, to create an ever-changing colour pattern.

Finally, using Microstation software, the architects again generated a more refined three-dimensional CAD representation of the body. Then, after fine-tuning the design, a new 1 : 100 scale maquette was computer numerically milled in clay - as illustrated in (fig. 6.6). This was then 'body-scanned' back into the computer for its ultimate digital existence.

At this point, the resolved structural model produced by Buro Happold was, like a hand being slipped into a glove, 'inserted' inside the Branson Coates 3D model. After a final review of their architectural and structural compatibility, the combined model was fed into a structural analysis program.

The Branson Coates design sequence for the Body Zone not only illustrates the importance of the physical model in architectural design and its role in design development, but it also exemplifies the role of the maquette in introducing more complex and challenging forms into the rationalising, digital space of the machine. This immersion of an evolving design idea in the dimensions of both physical and virtual space is becoming increasingly common practice. Indeed, returning from the 1999 UIA Congress in Beijing, Terry Farrell commented on how striking the similarity of design patterns has become in the leading practices, i.e.,beginning with provisional sketches and notes, then being pursued in three dimensions before being transferred for their analytical resolution in the computer. However, as we shall see, there are further stages and other benefits to be gained from this metamorphosis.

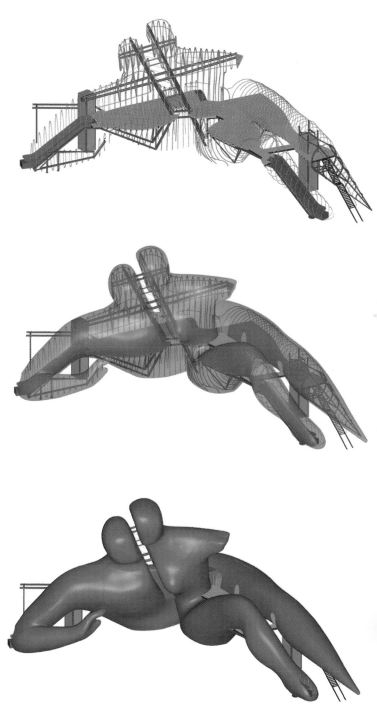

fig. 6.7 Body Zone Structure. Courtesy Branson Coates Architecture.

163

Over the years the designs of Frank O. Gehry have become increasingly more complex in form and more monumental in scale. Also, the office has grown to 120 people of which 90 are engaged in making models. Despite the plastic complexity of his buildings, however, all his projects continue to be born in sketches or conceived directly in three dimensions, i.e., evolved manually through successive generations of the now familiar design models (figs. 6.8a & 6.8b). Based on his contention that physical models and drawings are initially much faster at visualising new ideas, it is only later in the design process, when a concept has fully matured, that Gehry finally turns to the computer.

fig. 6.8b

fig. 6.8a

Samsung Museum of Modern Art design process model and design model: © Frank Gehry & Associates.

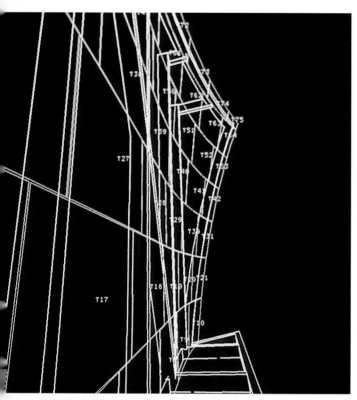

fig. 6.9 Catia analysis of stone wall, Walt Disney Concert Hall. © Frank Gehry & Associates.

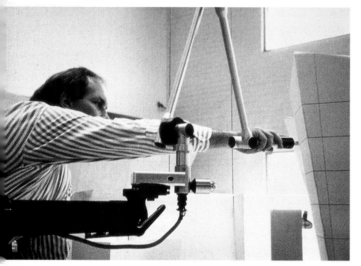

fig. 6.10 Faro Digitising Arm in action. © Frank Gehry & Associates.

Once this physical modelling process is exhausted, a physical model can then be scanned into the computer and digitised into an electronic version of itself (fig. 6.9). The scanning sequence is conducted with an articulated arm (incidentally, in an effort to improve on the scanning process Gehry & Associates have experimented with different equipment including Point Cloud scanners and even a CAT scanner) (fig. 6.10). Models are reconstructed as points and lines and then, using these references, surfaces are constructed. It is through the construction of the surfaces that the designers can 'rationalise' the model against a predetermined set of rules. This rationalisation process in the machine specifically relates to the intended construction technique and the materials to be employed in the final building. For example, the process might engage a set of rules for how a particular material may be bent or folded, or relate to some other aspect of the planned fabrication process, such as CADCAM fabrication limitations.

Running on IBM RISC 6000 computers, Gehry's practice uses the same Catia software as that developed by the French aerospace industry and later applied in the automative industry. It is Catia's ability in the planar modelling of non-polygonal surfaces that has been applied to several of Gehry's widely-published buildings, such as the stone cladding for the Disney Concert Hall in Los Angeles, the 'mosaic' of individually-shaped glazing for the steel and precast concrete facade of the Prague Office Building and, of course, for the titanium skin and, especially, the steel support structure of the Guggenheim Museum of Modern Art in Bilbao (fig. 6.11).

fig. 6.11 Guggenheim Museum, Bilbao. © Frank Gehry & Associates.

fig. 6.12 Stone wall mockup, Walt Disney Concert Hall. © Frank Gehry & Associates.

However, Gehry's adoption of this software is not to save time spent in design development but to increase the buildability of his technically challenging projects and, in response to the more complex geometries of his curving planes, to increase accuracy in the fabrication of more unforgiving building materials. For instance, to precisely machine the complex geometry of Gehry's more fluid planes in a modular system using, say, stone presents an enormous challenge. On the one hand, there is the need to achieve the level of accuracy necessary to eliminate unwanted interference and distortion in the apparently seamless curvature of a facade in which no two modular units are the same. On the other hand, the designers may seek repetition in, say, a component in a wall system. But this will depend upon the material, constructional system and desired technical and aesthetic being sought (fig. 6.12).

Consequently, Gehry's immersion of the physical model in the digitised and rationalising space of the computer - to re-emerge transformed in a new physical reality - is a process used both for design and cost control. Depending upon the technique used to electronically reconstitute the machined model, the reappearance of the physical form can involve different materials (fig.6.13).

For example, Gehry & Associates have used cut templates (contour modelling) either from paper or those cut by laser or waterjet. They have employed deposition machines for use with plastic and metal, and, in addition to a 3, 5 and 7 axis CNC milling machine, have also used an Helisys for producing laser cut contour models involving layers of paper.

fig. 6.13 CNC verification of Catia model in layered paper and resin. Der Neue Zollhof. © Frank Gehry & Associates.

fig. 6.14 Glazed tower fabrication. National Nederlanden Building. © Frank Gehry & Associates.

Apart from fine-tuning the design and detailing fabrication for suppliers, the Catia database is also used to generate construction documents for communication with contractors and subcontractors. In so doing, Gehry not only eases the transfer of the forms of his signature buildings into architectural existence but also streamlines the building process and, thereby, significantly reduces their overall cost (fig. 6.14).

William E. Massie

A CADCAM technology was also used in his Bozeman garage by William E. Massie, formerly a professor at Columbia University and now at the School of Architecture, Montana State University. Here, he produced a series of computer-generated drawings on 1/2" thick white PVC panels - the face of each being 'engraved' three-dimensionally in bas-relief by a flat-bed cutting machine connected to his computer. The panels were created as boards carrying his design submission for the Battle of the Little Big Horn Memorial competition (fig. 6.15). However, Massie's entry was quickly disqualified by the judges because the incisions into his panels were not deemed to exist as the kind of 'drawings' they had stipulated in the competition brief.

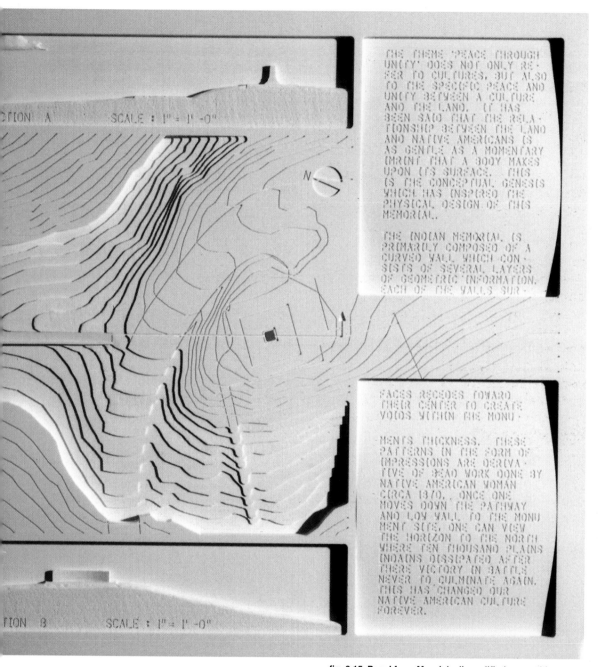

THE THEME 'PEACE THROUGH UNITY' DOES NOT ONLY RE-FER TO CULTURES, BUT ALSO TO THE SPECIFIC PEACE AND UNITY BETWEEN A CULTURE AND THE LAND. IT HAS BEEN SAID THAT THE RELA-TIONSHIP BETWEEN THE LAND AND NATIVE AMERICANS IS AS GENTLE AS A MOMENTARY IMPRINT THAT A BODY MAKES UPON ITS SURFACE. THIS IS THE CONCEPTUAL GENESIS WHICH HAS INSPIRED THE PHYSICAL DESIGN OF THIS MEMORIAL.

THE INDIAN MEMORIAL IS PRIMARILY COMPOSED OF A CURVED WALL WHICH CON-SISTS OF SEVERAL LAYERS OF GEOMETRIC INFORMATION. EACH OF THE WALLS SUR-

FACES RECEDES TOWARD THEIR CENTER TO CREATE VOIDS WITHIN THE MONU-

MENTS THICKNESS. THESE PATTERNS IN THE FORM OF IMPRESSIONS ARE DERIVA-TIVE OF BEAD WORK DONE BY NATIVE AMERICAN WOMAN CIRCA 1870. ONCE ONE MOVES DOWN THE PATHWAY AND LOW WALL TO THE MONU-MENT SITE, ONE CAN VIEW THE HORIZON TO THE NORTH WHERE TEN THOUSAND PLAINS INDAINS DISSIPATED AFTER THERE VICTORY IN BATTLE NEVER TO CULMINATE AGAIN. THIS HAS CHANGED OUR NATIVE AMERICAN CULTURE FOREVER.

fig. 6.15 Panel from Massie's disqualified competition entry.

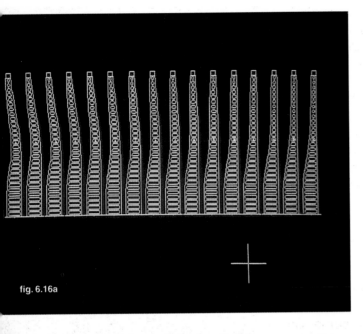

fig. 6.16a

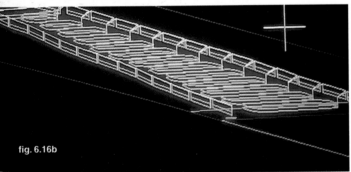

fig. 6.16b

Initial 3D computer model and wall sections (MasterCam).

Massie argues that we have been fixated for decades by an ideology that singularly focuses on all things retinal; the process of architectural design being long since severed from and outstripped by advances in technology. Even the spatial technology offered by the computer continues to be restricted to the role of visualiser and image-maker. However, while the general function of the computer has been relegated to the world of the 'virtual' and that of 'analysis', certain computer applications hold the potential of radically redefining our experience of an intellectual and physical space-making. Primarily developed in the automotive and aersopace industries for rapid prototyping and the fabrication of speciality parts, the advances in electronics and computer processing found in CNC technologies arrive to eradicate the gap between 'virtual' architectural propositions and the physical act of their construction. In other words, by eliminating drawings and opportunities for miscommunication and the gulf between thinking, imagining and actual construction, CNC advances provide the possibility of directly taking us from design conception to built form.

A further demonstration of the potential of CNC technology is found in Massie's AIA award-winning project conducted at the Montana State University. In order to test his idea of giving physicality to virtual mass, he initially conceived a biomorphic wall with dimensions of 9" thick x 7' wide x 7' high. First expressed as a three-dimensional CAD model in Microstation Triforma software, the computer model of Massie's non-rectilinear form was subsequently transferred to a second software package called MasterCam where it was manipulated, refined and 'sliced' into 32 vertical sections - each section being generated in cyberspace approximately 2.75" from its neighbour along the width of the wall (figs. 6.16a & 6.16b). The computer-modelled vertical sections were each composed of over 1,200 separate entities within the computer, none of which were identical, thus producing a continuously changing sequence of sections in which no two 'slices' were the same. So that the wall could be realised in the built environment, a tool path was created for each of the constituent sections. These were subsequently machined out of 3mm thick, air-impregnated PCV sheet material. The machined sections were then 're-assembled' on-site, reinforced internally with steel rods through specially machined slots, supported by formwork and covered with a continuous skin of taped acrylic applied in horizontal strips. Concrete was then injected into the residual void, filling the cavity and articulating what was, hitherto, a computer simulation of the wall. Finally, the exterior formwork and skin were removed to expose the complicated geometry of Massie's completed wall (fig. 6.17).

fig. 6.17 Formwork broken away and skin peeled back to reveal Massie's wall.

fig. 6.19 Diagrams of site geometry that drove the building design.

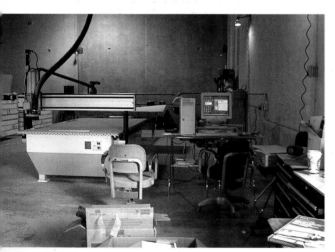

fig. 6.18 CNC milling machine setup in Massie's studio.

Apart from blurring the interface between the worlds of the virtual and the actual, the technology behind Massie's wall also points to a much wider architectural application. Inspired by the knowledge that Boeing have for some years already been engaged in building an aircraft entirely without drawings - going straight from computer to construction he realised that the technology had arrived at a point where he could bring it to architecture. Moreover, the cost of CNC equipment was falling: the CNC machine used by Massie that would have cost $250,000 a decade ago is now priced around $50,000 (fig. 6.18). Consequently, based on further research and employing Mastercam version 7 software to both design and machine the forms, Massie has already demonstrated this potential in the design and assembly of a full-scale housing unit sited in the sloping foothills of the Montana Big Belt Mountains.

But beyond economics, bringing this technology to architecture also required a different kind of thinking. Massie's work is an alchemy of the most advanced computer technology and of construction methods as basic as pouring concrete. It is a blending of architecture, art and invention. The process began with Massie studying the sight lines of the surroundings and, after a detailed survey, entering topographical data into his computer. 'I took the shape of the hills and put them into a computer model, Massie says, 'It's an attempt to develop an architecture that relates to the landscape'. However, to describe the resulting form as mirroring or matching the landscape does not quite capture the intention. Indeed, there was no intention to simulate the landscape. Rather, he was able to generate a more fluid spatial construct through what Massie calls 'visual rhyming'. For example, he explains that the words 'cat' and 'hat' embody entirely different meanings. But if one couples them as in a rhyme, a connection is formed. Similarly, when one creates a structure that relates to the landscape 'suddenly there's a kind of connection between those two events, i.e., a third aspect starts to exist'. In the case of the Big Belt Mountain site, Massie's 'visual rhyming' uses the geometries of 'foreground and background topographies' to both interrogate and integrate with the setting (fig. 6.19).

In equating cyberspace with a dimensionless and boundless 'ocean' of digital space, he describes the attendant lack of gravity and the multi-dimensional freedom of movement - the digitised version of his design in the computer enjoying a similar boundless expression due to the inconsequence of size or scale. For Massie the concept is purely spatial, and he contends that there is no major distinction between virtual and actual space - the forces and materials that intercept the design concept simply transforming it into a material existence. i.e., duplicating cyberspace with actual space. This is the moment when gravity, tactility, perception and the ability to physically circulate fuse into what we understand as architecture.

Produced entirely without the aid of orthographic drawings or physical prototypes, Massie defines this direct link between design and construction as 'the compression of idea to construct'. Employing a computer program developed for creating and machining complex curvature, he found that this software 'commodifies' the object by cutting a myriad single-directional slices through the computer model - a procedure that seriously questions the traditional design process. For instance, while the section drawing conventionally functions as an abstract view drawn for analytical purposes, the floor plan has always existed as the organisational or generating tool - a role famously underscored by Le Corbusier. However, in Massie's program, the section functions both as organisational and analytical design tool; the multi-sectional methodology, through variation and repetition, being the dominant means through which the space of the computer model is articulated (fig. 6.20).

fig. 6.20 CNC model of the support skeleton.

The preliminary, analytical digital slices were then reconfigured by Massie in the machine to generate the surface of the building, their digital codes being further deconstructed and manipulated into the primary and secondary components which, ultimately, would create the structure and the envelope of the building (fig. 6.21a & 6.21b). These slices amounted to some 1,015 unique components - the precision of the later machining process allowing their on-site assembly to be facilitated rather like a three-dimensional Chinese puzzle.

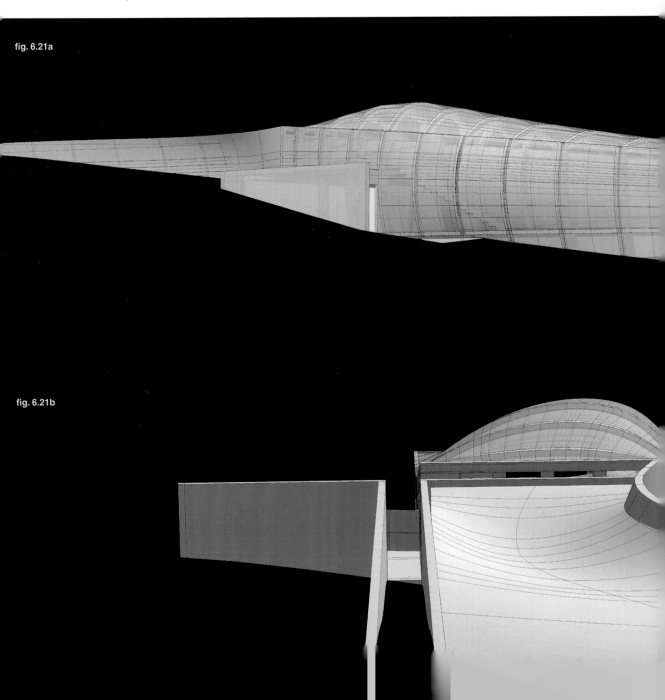

fig. 6.21a

fig. 6.21b

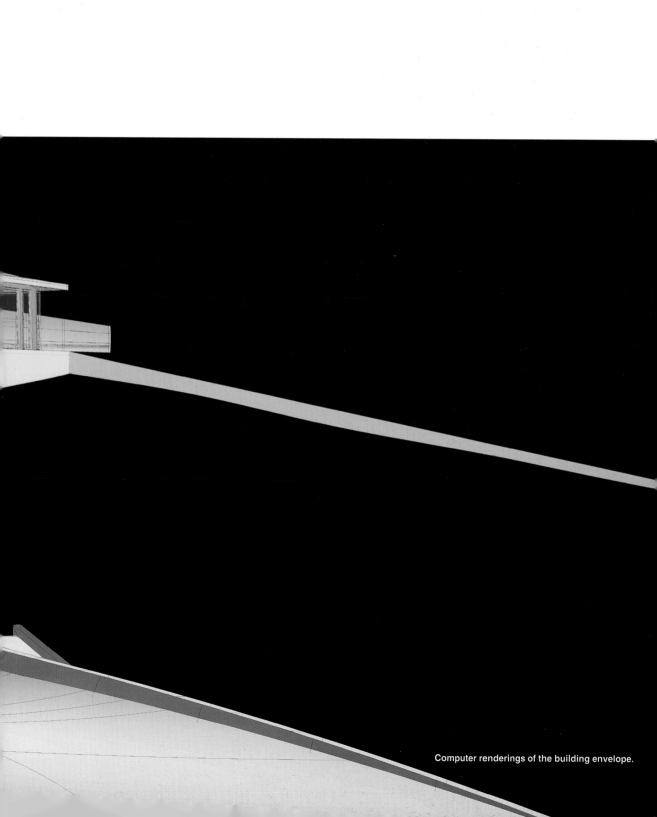

Computer renderings of the building envelope.

The initial construction process begins using Massie's CNC milling machine to cut forms out of foam. Each 3" thick form section is no bigger than 4 x 16' - the size of the foam sheets being used. The forms are then trucked to the site where they are pieced together. Steel structural reinforcing is added before concrete is pumped into the formwork to create a structural support for the building (figs. 6.22a , 6.22b, 6.22c & 6.22d). 'Doubters said it wouldn't work', says Massie, but he used a computer program to precisely engineer the exact location of every reinforcing bolt, ' . . . making the formwork super-intelligent'.

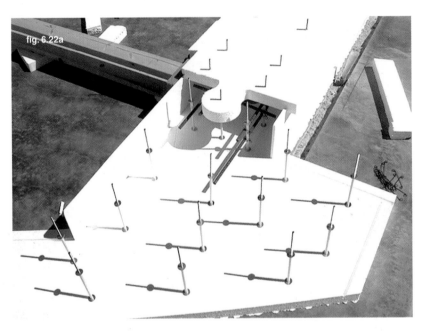

fig. 6.22a

fig. 6.22b

fig. 6.22c

fig. 6.22d

figs. 6.22a, 6.22b, 6.22c, 6.22d On-site construction.

By involving no construction documents, the computer-generated 'design code' eliminates the construction industry almost entirely from the design-construction process. For example, taking exactly the same time to cut out a straight line as it does a curved line, the machine does not value one over the other. Furthermore, one machine performs the function of an array of single-task machines used in the conventional fabrication of building components; thus eliminating the need to communicate a three- dimensional structure in its multiplicity of parts. Standardisation is also eliminated for, within a traditional building economy, designs are based on standardised building materials produced in standardised sizes. However, due to the meticulous precision involved in its assembly, an 8 x 4' mentality of a standardised set of rules is completely eradicated. The hardware and materials used in the fabrication of Massie's building form (computer cutting machine, steel, oriented strand board, concrete and foam) function at the interface between the virtual and actual worlds merely to mediate and give substance to the computer model. The result, Massie believes, exists as an example of the first actual building to embrace this process and methodology so completely (figs. 6.23 & 6.24).

fig. 6.23 Big Belt House interior.

fig. 6.24 Building in progress.

'The main objective is somewhat selfish' concludes Massie, 'The real aim is to produce a new form of architecture, but at the same time I'm very interested in having other people do the same kind of work. I would like to see architecture change as radically again as it did in the early part of the last century. That kind of change can occur again, and I am interested in pioneering this new technology'.

Michael Davis of the Richard Rogers Partnership has also described the way new technologies are currently transforming the way buildings look and function. He describes the best buildings of the future as interacting dynamically with both the user and with their immediate climate: 'More like robots than temples, these apparitions with their chameleon-like surfaces insist that we rethink the art of building'. Although Davis refers to the potential of 'smart' new materials, the promise of new technologies is further elaborated by the report *Construction: a 2020 Vision* published in April 1999. Based on interviews with over fifty leading construction specialists it predicts that, apart from instant CAD costing of buildings, and the satellite tracking of computer chip-embedded building components, the near future will see the replacement of on-site construction workers with robots. Building machines will assemble structures from top down - the top storey being jacked up while lower storeys are constructed beneath. The report concludes that two decades from now architects will still be designing buildings. Indeed, they will firmly remain in the driving seat; their designs driving the entire process - directly transferring from design to its physical realisation in the chosen building materials. Possibly, as Gehry and Massie already demonstrate, the architectural design process of the near future will not only visualise and develop itself at full scale in cyberspace but the resulting components that make up the building form will be seamlessly prototyped and mass-produced at full size by the machine before being robotically assembled on the site.

If this is the case, we then begin to envisage the coming of a new supermodel - a building idea, via the computer, moving directly from concept to construction. It is a vision in which the architect, the modelmaker and the builder of tomorrow may fuse as one to become the 'super-modelmaker'.